Third Curve

Saga of Women and Child
Development – Gujarat

Third Curve

Saga of Women and Child Development – Gujarat

Sandeep Singh

Viva Books

New Delhi | Mumbai | Chennai | Kolkata | Bengaluru | Hyderabad | Kochi | Guwahati

Publisher's note

The views and opinions expressed in this book are the author's own, and do not necessarily reflect the opinions subscribed to by the publisher.

Every possible effort has been made to ensure that the information contained in this book is accurate at the time of going to press, and the publisher and author cannot accept responsibility for any errors or omissions, however caused. No responsibility for loss or damage occasioned to any person acting, or refraining from action, as a result of the material in this publication can be accepted by the editor, the publisher or the author.

Every effort has been made to trace the owners of copyright material used in this book. The author and the publisher will be grateful for any omission brought to their notice for acknowledgement in the future editions of the book.

First Published 2014

Viva Books Private Limited

- 4737/23, Ansari Road, Daryaganj, New Delhi 110 002
  Tel. 42242200, 23258325, 23283121, Email: vivadelhi@vivagroupindia.net
- 76, Service Industries, Shirvane, Sector 1, Nerul, Navi Mumbai 400 706
  Tel. 022-27721273, 27721274, Email: vivamumbai@vivagroupindia.net
- Megh Tower, Old No. 307, New No. 165, Poonamallee High Road, Maduravoyal, Chennai 600 095
  Tel. 044-23780991, 23780992, 23780994, Email: vivachennai@vivagroupindia.net
- B-103, Jindal Towers, 21/1A/3 Darga Road, Kolkata 700 017
  Tel. 033-22816713, Email: vivakolkata@vivagroupindia.net
- 7, Sovereign Park Aptts., 56-58, K. R. Road, Basavanagudi, Bengaluru 560 004
  Tel. 080-26607409, Email: vivabangalore@vivagroupindia.net
- 101-102, Moghal Marc Apartments, 3-4-637 to 641, Narayanguda, Hyderabad 500 029
  Tel. 040-27564481, Email: vivahyderabad@vivagroupindia.net
- First Floor, Beevi Towers, SRM Road, Kaloor, Kochi 682 018
  Tel. 0484-2403055, 2403056, Email: vivakochi@vivagroupindia.net
- 232, GNB Road, Beside UCO Bank, Silpukhuri, Guwahati 781 003
  Tel. 0361-2666386, Email: vivaguwahati@vivagroupindia.net

www.vivagroupindia.com

ISBN: 978-81-309-2592-9

Published by Vinod Vasishtha for Viva Books Private Limited, 4737/23, Ansari Road, Daryaganj, New Delhi 110 002.

Printed and bound by Syndicate Binders, New Delhi.

SUB-0022

Yatra Naryastu Poojyante,
Ramante Tatra Devata – Manusmriti 3.56

Where women are worshipped, Gods dwell

Contents

Acknowledgment

Any book is not possible without the help of many people. This book is no exception. This book wouldn't have been possible without the support of Government of Gujarat, Department of Information, Department of Women and Child Development and its officials. I will remain grateful to them. I also had the support of many friends. I extend my thanks to them.

As it is said that books are man's best friend, I had the support of quite a few books which I must acknowledge here. '***Emotional Design***' by Donald A. Norman, '***Emotional Intelligence and Working with Emotional Intelligence***' by Daniel Goleman, '***The Cycle of Leadership***' by Noel M. Tichy with Nancy Cardwell, '***Judgment***' by Noel M. Tichy and Warren G. Bennis and Designing and Creating '***Second Curve***' Healthcare Systems by Ted Ball, Martin D. Merry, M.D. and Liz Verlaan-Cole. I have borrowed some sentences from these friends to express my thoughts. A detailed reference is given at the end of the book. If I have left any reference, then it would be only because of oversight.

In the 'Introduction' section readers will find a mention where the Chief Minister of Gujarat, Shri Narendra Modi is addressing me as Sandeep 'Bhai'. This is not an attempt to claim familiarity with, but, it is a standard practice of addressing any adult male in Gujarat as Bhai (brother), while female adults are addressed as Ben (sister). But I must admit that, a conversation with him has resulted in this book.

Data, Statistics used in the book are from Government of Gujarat, if taken from any other source, the source has been duly acknowledged. For any conclusions drawn or views expressed in this book, unless specifically attributed to anyone else, the responsibility is entirely mine.

– ***Sandeep Singh***

Preface

Gujarat Chief Minister Narendra Modi was in Dwarka, where he met a group of local women. He asked how many of them were educated. The women over 80 years raised their hands while many of the younger women did not. This is the usual pattern in most parts of India. The reason why all the older women of Dwarka were educated was that they grew up in the erstwhile Kingdom of Baroda, ruled by the Great Sayajirao Gaekwad III. Primary education was compulsory in the state for boys and girls after 1906, many decades before independence. Sayajirao encouraged men of the stature of B.R. Ambedkar, Aurobindo Ghosh and Sarvepalli Radhakrishnan at the beginning of their careers.

The quest to build a modern India began in those decades, and progressive rulers such as Sayajirao were linked to this quest. India in the last decades of the 19th century was rediscovering its roots as well as yearning for a modern future.

Post independence, the Indian renaissance was halted in its track. S.S. Gill wrote in his book 'Dynasty': "...Nehru often showed impatience at the slow progress of various development schemes. But as to education he stated: 'Education is spreading fairly well and today we have some fifty million boys and girls in our schools and colleges.' And he was still more elated about the state of women's education. He wrote: 'Already I see major changes taking place which are not perhaps so evident to outsiders. Probably the biggest revolution that is taking place in India is through women's education which affects directly home.'"

What was the basis of this optimism? Female literacy crawled from 8 to 16 per cent between the census of 1951 and 1961: a measly rise of 8% percentage points in 10 years – and that too from such a low base. Yet, somehow Nehru appears to have convinced himself that this was the 'biggest revolution that is taking place in India.'

In the book 'Subhas Chandra Bose – Pioneer of Indian Planning' published by Planning Commission, in 1997 Deputy Chairman of Planning Commission, Madhu Dandavate wrote:

"The blueprint for Free India outlined by Netaji Subhas Chandra Bose in his presidential address at the Haripura session of the Indian National Congress in February 1938, envisaged that the first task of the Government of Free India would be to set up a 'National Planning Commission'. ...Having talked of importance of National Planning at Haripura in February 1938, Netaji ensured before the year was out, that the 'National Planning Committee' was inaugurated by him on December 17, 1938. Netaji appointed Pandit Jawaharlal Nehru as the first Chairman of this committee. This National Planning Committee later was succeeded by the Advisory Planning Board set up by the Interim Government in 1946. Subsequently in Free India, the Planning Commission, as it is known today, was constituted in 1952.

When I joined as the Deputy Chairman of the Planning Commission, I recollected Netaji's writing on National Planning and realized that much of what he had advocated was still to be translated into reality."

The statements of S.S. Gill and Madhu Dandavate is truly reflected when one looks at the Women and Child Development in the Five Year Plans of India.

Women and men in India enjoy de jure equality. Article 14 of the Constitution of India guarantees equal rights and opportunities to men and women in political, economic and social spheres, Article 42 directs the State to make provision for ensuring just and humane conditions for work and maternity itself and Article 51A (e) imposes upon every citizen, a fundamental duty to renounce the practices derogatory to the dignity of women.

However this de jure equality has not yet materialised into a de facto equality, despite the efforts made in the Five Year Plans.(Table-1)

Perspective on Advancement of Women through Five Year Plans

Five Year Plan (1951-56)	It was mainly welfare oriented as far as women's issue were concerned. The Central Social Welfare Board (CSWB) undertook a number of welfare measures through the voluntary sector. The programmes for women were implemented through the National Extension Service Programmes through Community Development Blocks.
Second Five Year Plan (1956-61)	Efforts were geared to organize 'Mahila Mandals' (women's group) at grass-roots levels to ensure better implementation of welfare schemes.
Third, Fourth, Fifth & other Interim Plans (1961-79)	They accorded high priority to women's education. Measures to improve maternal and child health services and supplementary feeding for children, nursing and expectant mothers were also introduced.
Sixth Five Year Plan (1980-85)	This is regarded as a landmark in women's development. The Plan adopted a multidisciplinary approach with a three-pronged thrust on health, education and employment of women.
Seventh Five Year Plan (1985-90)	Development programmes for women were continued, with the objective of raising their economic and social status and bring them into the mainstream of national development. A very significant step therein was to identify and promote 'beneficiary-oriented programmes' which extended direct benefits to women.
Eighth Five Year Plan (1992-97)	It attempted to ensure that the benefits of development from different sectors did not bypass women. Special programmes were implemented to complement the general development programmes. The flow of benefits to women in the three core sectors of education, health and employment were monitored vigilantly. Women were enabled to function as equal partners and participants in the developmental process with reservation in the membership of local bodies. This approach of the Eighth Plan marks a definite shift from 'development to empowerment' of women.

Ninth Five Year Plan (1998-2002)	The Ninth Five Year Plan envisaged: **a)** Empowerment of women and socially disadvantaged groups such as Scheduled Castes. Scheduled Tribes and Other Backward Classes and Minorities as agents of socio-economic change and development. **b)** Promoting and developing peoples participatory institution like Panchayti Raj institutions, cooperatives and self-help groups. **c)** Strengthening efforts to build self-reliance. **d)** The convergence of services from different sectors. **e)** A women's component plan at the Central and State levels.
Tenth Five Year Plan (2002-07)	The Tenth Five Year Plan was formulated to ensure requisite access of women to information, resources and services and advance gender equality goals.
Eleventh Five Year Plan (2007-12)	The Eleventh Five Year Plan proposes to undertake special measures for gender empowerment and equity. The Ministry of Women and Child Development would make synergistic use of gender budget and gender mainstreaming process.

(Table-1) India, Planning Commission, (2002) Five Year Plan, New Delhi; www.nipccd.nic.in

The First Five Year Plan sought to 'promote the welfare of women' by helping them to play their legitimate role in the family and the community but emphasised that the major burden of organising activities for the benefit of the female population had to be borne by the private agencies. Five Year Plans continued to reflect the same welfare approach to women's interests though they accorded priority to education for both, men and women and launched measures to improve maternal and child health services and supplementary nutrition for children as well as expectant and nursing mothers.

It was the Sixth Five Year Plan in which the focus on women's interests shifted from 'welfare' and 'development'. Planners and policy makers began to recognize women not only as partners but also as stake-holders in the development of the country. The Seventh Five Year Plan saw developmental programs which aimed at raising the economic and social status of women and at ensuring that they get the benefits of national development. This is when 'beneficiary oriented programs' extending direct benefits to women in different developmental sectors began. There was a stress upon the generation of both skilled and unskilled employment through formal and non-formal education and vocational training.

The Eighth Five Year Plan had a Human Development focus. It tried to ensure that the benefits of development do not bypass women and it implemented special programs for women to complement the general development programs and to monitor the flow of benefits to women in education, health and employment.

The Ninth Five Year Plan took up 'empowering women as agents of socio-economic change and development' as a major commitment. To begin with, it adopted the 'National Policy for Empowerment of Women', which among other objectives, sought to organise women into Self Help Groups to work for their own empowerment, accorded a high priority to schemes for maternal and child welfare and most importantly, made a bid at easy and equal access to education through the Special Action Plan of 1998, plans for the free education of girls up to the college level (inclusive of professional courses) and vocational training.

The Tenth Five Year Plan was formulated to ensure advance gender equity goals. While the Eleventh Five Year Plan thought of making synergistic use of gender budget and gender mainstreaming process.

Five Year Plans sum up the government of India's initiative on the Women and Child Development, since 1947.

Apart from Government of India's initiative, in terms of the women's movement there have been divergent understandings of oppression and its outcomes and, hence different strategies to combat it. Some initiatives have been by intellectual groups; while, there have been some that have had mass support. Some have emerged in support of certain causes or for the purpose of a focused campaign, while there are some that have existed for years with evolving agendas. The ideologies also vary from radical, liberal, socialist, and Marxist to Gandhian.

According to Mazumdar (2000), the women's movement's engagement with the law can be divided into two wings, namely, the 'Rights Wing' and the 'Empowerment Wing'. The former refers to those who have targeted their demands on the state and seek legislative mandates for women's advancement, while the latter refers to those who place more emphasis on empowering women from 'within' themselves. However, one cannot make such a clear distinction in reality, as even within those who might largely fall under the first group, namely, the 'Rights Wing', there might be sections that question the implementation of the very law that has been demanded. Therefore, another school of thought has co-existed within the women's movement that has questioned the role of the law in social transformation (Desouza 2007).

Some feminists have taken the debate a step further to attribute the law as a symbol of patriarchy. They argue that most often laws are framed by men, the legal interpretations are male centric, there are prevailing gender biases amongst the law enforcers and gender stereotypes built into the courtroom procedures which, therefore, make one's confidence in the law seem questionable.

None of the issues of the women's movement in the 20th century in India have ceased to be concerns of the women in 21st century. In fact, some issues have become rather complex with social developments that are taking place.

The changes or transitions that have brought about women's development in India have not followed a chronological pattern. Every State Government has its own plan along with the Union Governments.

Within the state of Gujarat the budget provision for women and child development during the last five years has been increased by more than 400% from Rs. 297.83 crore in 2006-07 to Rs. 1280.89 crore in 2011-12. One can safely conclude that this money has been well spent; when one comes to know that in order to ensure that services are delivered to the remotest centers of the State, GIS mapping has been done of Anganwadi centers.

In the television serial 'Yes, Minister,' in one of the episodes the Minister, full of reforming zeal, tries to figure out from the immovable permanent secretary, Sir Humphrey, how many women are in really senior positions in the British civil service. Sir Humphrey says that it is very difficult to give an exact number; it would require a lot of investigation. The Minister is still insistent, and wants to know approximately how many women are there in these senior positions. "Approximately, none," Sir Humphrey replies.

Well, 25% of Gujarat Government employees are females (Annexure-1). Graph-I depicts the number of male and female employees in the Department of Education and Department of Health & Family Welfare.

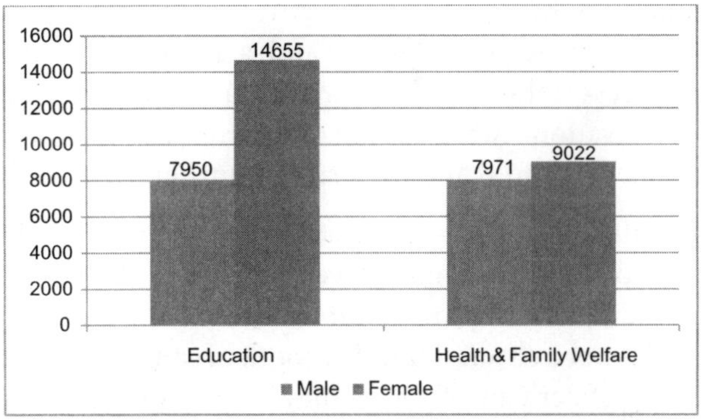

Male and Female Employee in Gujarat Government, (Graph-I)

One of the reasons of high female employment is naturally because women feel safe. Gujarat is the most secure for women as per the Female Security Index of Tata Strategic Management Group's 2013 report on 'Well Being and Female Security in India', which is based on 3 categories: a) Gender ratio in 0-6 years age group, b) Incidence of rape and c) Dowry deaths.

Going by the various reports in media and awards it becomes obvious that the best place for women to be in India is Gujarat. Let's look at some of the awards and excerpts from the news:

Ahmedabad District Panchayat has received an award for fighting malnutrition in rural areas. The D.L. Shah Award for general services in government category was bestowed upon the Ahmedabad District Panchayat by the Quality Council of India during its 8th National Quality Conclave held on March 8-9, 2013 in New Delhi. The award was conferred upon the panchayat on the basis of coverage, innovativeness, reliability and sustainability.

The Economic Times on 22 March 2012 reported that "Narendra Modi's Gujarat has many celebrated firsts to its credit but what the public relations team might have missed out on is an experiment with technology that appears to be bearing fruit. With a few million mobile connections and a thousand-odd health workers, Gujarat sought to reduce avoidable child and maternity-linked deaths, and had some success in a short span of two years prompting the central government to adopt it across the country."

Chiranjeevi Scheme of Gujarat government has been emulated by eight other states governments and a further barometer of the program's success is the coveted awards it has won – amongst them are the Asian Innovation Award at Singapore from the *Wall Street Journal* and the *Financial Express* and the Prime Minister's Award, 2009.

Friends, this book is an attempt to take the readers through the process of Women and Child Development in Gujarat. It is about programs and leadership in Women and Child Development in Gujarat. This is not a chronological account of campaigns and schemes, but yes, it is a statement of the 'achievements' of the programs; it is an attempt to sketch the evolution of the thought process and the transitions within it. Gujarat has followed a path breaking model of development. My idea is not to dole out statistics to substantiate it. Women and Child Development in Gujarat has gone way beyond statistics and become an established model that needs to be emulated without any doubt. As they say:

"*Haath kangan ko aarsi kya, padhe likhe ko farsi kya*".

i.e.

Haath mein pehne hue kangan dekhne ke liye darpan ki jaroorat nahi. Isi tarah jo baat saaf samne nazar aa rahi ho to uski parakh ke liye khoj kya karni.

i.e.

One doesn't need a mirror for the ornaments in forearm,
one is expected to know Farsi if one calls himself educated...

Introduction

One day in November 2011, I along with Dewang Nanavati and Vijay Chauthaiwale was off to Gandhinagar to meet the man, whom I always wanted to meet; Shri Narendra Modi, the Chief Minister of Gujarat. It was a Sunday, and the man who has given a new dimension to development in India was working.

The meeting started and the Chief Minister started sharing his development initiatives, one after the other, the thought behind the initiatives, the results, the statistics, the future plans. It was like listening to a dotting proud father explaining achievements of his kids. We didn't realize when one and half hours passed by.

I have never met a Chief Minister or Minister, either at State or Central level so passionate about development (I had the fortune to meet quite a few). But what struck me about the Chief Minister Narendra Modi was the honesty or should I say brutal honesty.

One thought that stands out in my mind is Chief Minister Narendra Modi's example of a scheme for widows. Chief Minister Narendra Modi said: "Government of Gujarat gives sewing machine and training to widows. One day I called the IAS officers, responsible for the program in the districts and asked them, are they aware of the program of giving sewing machine to widows? They all said yes. Then I gave all the officers a piece of paper and asked them to write, how a women who has become a widow should go about to get the sewing machine."

Chief Minster said: "Sandeep bhai you will be surprised, that, no one could answer it."

Chief Minister went on, "then I called ministers, and asked them are they aware of the program of giving sewing machine to widows.

They all said yes. Then I gave all the ministers a piece of paper and asked them to write, how a women who has become a widow should go about to get the sewing machine."

Chief Minster again said, "Sandeep bhai you will be surprised, that, no one could answer it."

The best was yet to come.

Chief Minister then said, "Sandeep Bhai you will be shocked, even I didn't know."

Then Chief Minister said, "I thought if IAS officers, Ministers and Chief Minister don't know then how will a widow know. When a women has lost her husband she will be in a very miserable state of mind herself; she will have to pull herself up and look after her kids and family responsibility. Government programs being run for her benefit may not come in her mind almost upto a year of her widowhood?"

After this experience Chief Minister Chief Minister decided that a widow will not come to the government but the government will go to the widow.

Now, this is how the scheme works in Gujarat. The widow scheme is promoted on a priority basis through meetings, pamphlets and word of mouth to name a few. The employee at Gram Sabha has the form and details. (Annexure-2A & 2B) One of the successful beneficiaries of the scheme is:

Amtulla Ikbalbhai Daudivohra, of Chuda, Surendranagar, a 29 year-old widow. When her husband died, she was not employed and had little formal education. She was helpless and desperate for work. Someone in her village told her about the widow training scheme. She has never looked back since.

Once the training was over she received financial support of Rs. 5,000/- with which she started a small shop in her village. She says, "It is a novelty item store, I earn about Rs. 3,000-5,000/- per month from it. The practical knowledge imparted during the training proved to be very helpful."

Amtullaben says, "I am very happy that the Government is running such a scheme that makes us financially independent."

Chief Minister Narendra Modi's brutal honesty about the lack of knowledge about the government procedure in himself, his colleagues and his officers is reflected in government documents, which clearly states that the sex ratio in the state is low as far as females are concerned. It is a significant step, because generally governments try to hide facts. (Lack of awareness of governmental procedure within government will be true for all governments but admitting the same and improving on it can happen only under Chief Minister Narendra Modi's leadership).

It also reminds of Emotional Intelligence. Emotional Intelligence does not mean merely 'being nice, at strategic moments it may demand not 'being nice'. Emotional Intelligence also does not mean giving free rein to feelings – letting it all hang out. Rather it means managing feelings so that they are expressed appropriately and effectively, enabling people to work together smoothly towards their common goal. Leaders constantly look for opportunities to explain how a decision or a choice fits into the overall strategy because often those small points are the best illustrations of the larger picture. Instances like this become 'Moments of Truth' for any good organization.

Aristotle said, "Anyone can become angry – that is easy. But to be angry with the right person, to the right degree, at the right time, for the right purpose, and in the right way – this is not easy." This is where, Chief Minister Narendra Modi stands out. A leader's most important role in any organisation is in making good judgments – being well informed, taking wise decisions that produce the desired outcomes. The judgment of the Chief Minister Narendra Modi can be appreciated in its true context when one understands the following:

One's passion when well exercised, have wisdom; they guide the thinking, the values, and the decisions. But they can easily go awry, and do so all too often. As per Aristotle, the problem is not with emotionality, but with the appropriateness of emotion and its expression.

Narendra Modi combines intelligence and emotions in his judgment.

The women's development has a long history in India. Much longer than the current 'second wave' movement, or even the 'first wave' of earlier this century. The Shakti cults goes back centuries, and the concept of Shakti – the female power principle – was recognized thousands of years ago. In this form the women's movement represents not merely an oppositional force fuelled by anger, a rather negative reaction to oppression, but the development of a distinctive female culture, a positive creative force inspiring men and women alike (Liddle et al. 1986: 5).

Yet Aradhana Sharma in 'Paradoxes of Empowerment' writes, "First the government used (women) for votes (as the vote banks), and then it used us for sloganeering. Then NGOs used us for protests against alcohol, in the Sarvodaya movement, in forest protection movements. Once they have used us, they tell us to back off and go back (to our usual existence). This has always happened. When they needed Shakti (female power), the Gods created Kali (the Hindu goddess who personifies Shakti). And when she did what she was supposed to do, she was told to go and sit in a temple. 'Now, you are not needed; now people will worship you and you can be happy.' And she was locked up in a temple."

Unfortunately, Aradhana Sharma is not entirely wrong.

- Couple of years ago, when, Soumya, a young lady TV reporter in New Delhi was murdered on her way home late at night after duty in New Delhi, the Chief Minister of New Delhi, Ms Sheila Dixit deplored the fact that young women should be so 'adventurous'.
- The Class XI student, who was brutally assaulted by a mob of more than 50 men in public at Guwahati, had to face more humiliation when her identity was revealed first by Alka Lamba from fact-finding team of National Commission for Women (NCW) and then by Assam Chief Minister Tarun Gogoi's office.

Fortunately we have exception in the form of State of Gujarat and its Chief Minister Narendra Modi. Under his leadership literacy level has gone up by 12.93% in a decade. Increase in female literacy is not a stand-alone phenomenon; it depends on various factors like women's health, time in hand etc. Let me illustrate this by one example. The supply of tapped water has increased to 74% from earlier 4%. Now the time and energy saved in fetching the water would have been used productively somewhere, and definitely literacy would have been one of them. I don't have a study linking the two, but commonsense makes one believe in this.

Chief Minister Narendra Modi has worked hard to get the women their Shakti back. Not surprising, that for Chief Minister Narendra Modi the Goddess came out from the temple and the results are visible. *The Times of India* on 6 April 2011 reported news by Pramod Panwar, "Ambaji temple takes up fight against child malnutrition". "Ambaji temple will be providing fruits and nutritious food as part of its *prasad* distribution to malnourished children of Banaskantha district through the mid-day meal programme. These kids could number nearly 4 lakh," said Banaskantha collector R.J. Patel, who is also ex-officio chairman of Ambaji Temple Trust.

"According to the 2001 census, around 70 per cent of children in the district are chronically malnourished in remote places of Danta, Amirgadh and western talukas on the international border of Banaskantha district. The Ambaji temple had therefore launched a project to check malnutrition whose typical outward signs are swollen bellies, listlessness and dull eyes. The fruits and food will come from well-off devotees of Goddess Amba, Patel said on Wednesday. *Prasad* of the temple will comprise fruits such as mangoes, bananas, orange, pineapples and other condiments offered to Goddess Amba and will be supplied to different taluka places for distribution at mid-day meal centers. This project will continue round the year," Patel said. "Under the project, the devotees will offer *prasad* only in the form of fruits or milk, sweets and other nourishing condiments, but not cash," he said.

Gujarat is a state where not only women's project but the efforts are aimed to bring qualitative changes in the life of a common man with the following Panchamrut Philosophy:

1. Jan Shakti
2. Gyan Shakti
3. Urja Shakti
4. Jal Shakti
5. Rakshan Shakti

All the major development initiatives are part of the above mentioned Five Programs. The development of the state surrounded around Shakti, emerges from the fact that a woman is the nucleus around whom the family, the society and the whole community moves. The development of the community cannot be separated or viewed in isolation from the development of women. Their contribution in the home and their work outside the home makes them important and indispensable agents of our society for bringing about social change.

Now let's look at the nomenclature of the programs. Names are all about emotions. And emotions are all about judgment. Without understanding, people have no idea what to do when things go wrong – and things do go wrong. The secret to good understanding is to establish a proper conceptual model. In *The Design of Everyday Things*, Donald A. Norman pointed out that there are three different mental images of any object. First is the image in the head of the designer – call that the 'designer's model.' Then the image that the person using the device has of it and the way it works: call this the 'user's model.' In an ideal world, the designer's model and the user's model should be identical and, as a result, the user understands and uses the item properly. Alas, designers don't talk to the final users; they only specify the product. People form their models entirely from their observations of the product – from its appearance, how it operates, what feedback it provides, and perhaps, any accompanying written material, such as the advertising and manuals. Donald A. Norman called the image conveyed by the product and written material the 'system image.'

Designers can communicate with the eventual users only through the system image of a product, Thus, a good designer will make sure that the system image of the final design conveys the proper user model. Chief Minister Narendra Modi has been able to do the same by naming the program 'SHAKTI'.

The initiative had begun long before naming of programs. In 2001, Chief Minister Narendra Modi, for the empowerment of women, social, educational and economic development of women, initiated Department of Women and Child Development with the thought of giving the much needed impetus to the holistic development of women and children. The aim was not only welfare but also the development and empowerment of women.

Women's adolescent and adult years are the time when women strive to fulfill their potential for their lives, their families and communities, and their societies. Since childbearing is a key part of these years for most women in developing countries, maternal health has an important impact on their ability to 'deliver', in every way. Maternal health most directly affects a women's own health and survival and that of her new born. However maternal health is linked to women's lives not simply as health issue. As an individual in her own right, women's status and empowerment as an individual and her ability to be a healthy mother strongly impact each other. As a member of a family, the health and well being of a mother shape the health and education of her children and the finances and welfare of her household. Finally at a macro level, poor maternal health strongly affects a nation's economic development.

Women's Different Roles and Participation in Development with key linkages as per the background paper for the Women Deliver Conference 2007 is as follows:

- ***Women as Citizens:***

  Macro-level Development Effects

  - Growth
  - Productivity
  - Equity
  - Burden of Disease
  - Health Service Delivery

- ***Women as Family Members:***
  Micro-level Development Effects
  - Child Health
  - Child Education
  - Household Finances
  - Family Well Being
- ***Women as Mothers:***
  Maternal Health
  - Maternal Mortality & Morbidity
  - Newborn Mortality & Morbidity
- ***Women as Individuals:***
  Other Aspects of Women's Status
  - Education
  - Economic Opportunity
  - Decision Making
  - Reproductive Health

The above is reflected in different departments created, under the aegis of Department of Women and Child Development, which are mentioned below:

Integrated Child Development Services: Launched on 2nd October 1975, ICDS Scheme represents one of the world's largest and most unique programs for early childhood development. Gujarat has emerged as a guiding State for many states within India by reaching out ICDS service to 18,500 villages.

Gujarat State Commission for Women: Under the Gujarat State Commission for Women Act 2002, State Government with their major objectives of encouraging women's rights along with their social, economic and educational development initiated this commission in 2005.

Gujarat Women Economic Development Corporation: To address the issue of women who are socially and financially weak and for their upliftment, in 1981 Gujarat Women Economic Development Corporation was established and registered under Company's Act 1956.

Gender Resource Center: Established in 2003, to provide support for incorporating gender equity and equality in overall development process and plans of the state.

Social Defense: For the purpose of security and rehabilitation of needy women, Directorate of Social Defense was established. Under this through social security department and Gujarat Women Economic Development Corporation, required assistance and guidance in handling 10 governmental and 11 non-governmental organizations. Further through Social Defense women centric acts like Dowry Act, Prevention of Domestic Violence Act 2005, Immoral Traffic (Prevention) Act, 1986 and Prohibition of Child Marriage Act 2006 etc. are also being implemented.

Women's Wing: One of the main roles of Women's Wing is to manage Multipurpose Women Welfare Centers. They run the women helpline no. 18002331111.

Designing Want Based Programs

The distinction between needs and wants is what is truly necessary for a person's life and livelihood versus what a person asks for. Satisfying people's true needs, including the requirements of different cultures, gender, age groups, social and national requirements, is not only difficult but is a major challenge. To some leaders, the challenge seems overwhelming. To others, it inspires.

To the leaders who practice human-centered program, serving people means relieving them of frustration, of confusion, of a sense of helplessness; to make people empowered and in their own control, take care of both their need and want.

If people don't really know what they want, then it is very difficult to satisfy their needs? In the case of human-centered design (human centered design takes care of both need and want), it is to provide people with the tools to explore by themselves, to try this and that, to empower themselves to success. To politicians, just the reverse is true. For them this is an opportunity to present themselves as rescuers 'in-shining-armor,' ready to offer assistance, to provide just the answer people will be led to believe they had been seeking.

It is like Shopping Malls who put the most frequently desired items at the rear of the store, forcing buyers to pass by isles of tempting impulse purchases. If government is a shopping mall whose different programs are like the products then political leaders are the clever salesman, beneficiary the customer and, bribe takes the form of impulse purchase.

It needs a leader, not merely a politician to design government programs in such a way that it can satisfy both the needs and wants of its subjects. The human centered design originates in the mind, in the brain. Let us look at some of the 'want based programs.'

Launched in Amreli in the December of 2009, the Garib Kalyan Mela is the Chief Minister's initiative to bring about transparency between government and its people of the state. The scheme focuses on the poorest of the poor in the state in an effort to bring about a financial inclusion of these people in the economy of the state. Providing benefits on the spot to the people present at the mela, this action oriented schemes removes the middleman. The main cause of concern, it has been established is the presence of such middleman who pretend to act as interface between the ignorant and the government and fleece the poor out of their due benefits. In an effort to make the government more proactive and pro people, it was decided to take the benefits to the poor rather than wait for the poor to claim their benefits. This has worked wonders. (Table-2)

The entire scheme has been broken down to various levels and sub levels in order to ensure the percolation of benefits to the lowest level of society. Taluka level teams have been formed under the chairmanship of Class I officers and the proceedings in every taluka are monitored on a weekly basis. The Garib Kalyan melas are held at local levels of every taluka and municipality. In the build-up leading to these melas, all secretaries have to allocate district wise targets. This is done along with weekly taluka level meetings organised by the Chairman of taluka level committees. A list of beneficiaries is identified by all the Collectors and DDOs. The districts officials then identify process, scrutinize and sanction cases under individual oriented programs and schemes. The release of advance funds is done via fixed deposits as per requirements of the department. The disbursement of the financial benefits is then carried out, and the beneficiaries receive their benefits at the Garib Kalyan Mela itself, in an on-the-spot procedure. After the process is over, the names of the beneficiaries are displayed at the village panchayat office. This sort of proactiveness and transparency has resulted in establishing a successful method of disseminating help to the people who need it the most.

No. of Women Benefited from Garib Kalyan Melas (2010-11)		
S. No.	**Type of Benefit**	**No. of Women**
1	Housing	2,03,832
2	Employment	2,43,783
3	Agriculture	49,361
4	Social Security	50,239
5	Women & Child Welfare	2,87,867
6	Social Welfare	59,021
7	Other Support Schemes	4,93,415

(Table-2)

So far more than 32 lakh women have been given assistance in Garib Kalyan Melas of which about 6.5 lakhs have benefited under employment schemes.

Donald A. Norman's studies of emotion, conducted with his colleagues Andrew Ortony and William Revelle, professors in the Psychology Department at Northwestern University, suggest that the human attributes result from three different levels of the brain:

- the automatic, prewired layer, called the *visceral level*;
- the part that contains the brain processes that control everyday behavior, known as the *behavioral level*; and
- the contemplative part of the brain, or the *reflective level.*

Each of these three brain level plays a critical role in human behavior, each an equally critical role in the design, marketing, and use of products. Human responses to the everyday things of the world are complex, and determined by a wide variety of factors. Some of these are outside the individual, controlled by designer and manufacturer, or by advertising, brand image. And some come from within, from the individual's own, private experiences. Each of the three levels of design-visceral, behavioral, and reflective – plays its part in shaping individual's experience. Each is as important as the others, but each requires a different approach by the designer.

Similarly each level produces a different style of program. But first let us understand the three brain levels a bit more as explained by Norman.

Visceral design is what nature does. Humans evolved to coexist in the environment of other humans, animals, plants, landscapes, weather, and other natural phenomena. As a result, we are exquisitely tuned to receive powerful emotional signals from the environment that get interpreted automatically at the visceral level. Hence, Visceral design concerns itself with appearances. The visceral level is fast: it makes rapid judgments of what is good or bad, safe or dangerous, and sends appropriate signals to the muscles (the motor system) and alerts the rest of the brain. This is the start of affective processing.

Behavioral design has to do with the pleasure and effectiveness of use. The behavioral level is the site of most human behavior. Action at that level can be enhanced or inhibited by the reflective layer and, in turn, it can enhance or inhibit the visceral layer. What matters here are four components of good behavioral design: function, understandability, usability, and physical feel.

The highest layer is that of reflective thought. Note that it does not have direct access either to sensory input or to the control of behavior. Instead it watches over, reflects upon, and tries to bias the behavioral level. Reflective design covers a lot of territory. It is all about message, about culture, and about the meaning of a program or its use.

Visceral, behavioral, and reflective: These three very different dimensions are interwoven through any product or program design. It is not possible to have design without all three, but their domination varies from program to program.

The different programs for Women and Child Development by the Government of Gujarat can be classified into three categories as per their dominant design. Table-3 lists some of the programs:

Visceral Design	Behavioral Design	Reflective Design
Balika Samruddhi Yojna	Fish Entrepreneur Yojna	Beti Bachao
Multipurpose Women Welfare Centers	Krishi Talim Yojna	Nari Adalat
Swayamsidh Yojna	Kunverbai nu Mameru Scheme	
	Mahila Vrudh Ashram	
	Saat Phera Samuh Yojna	

	Sakhi Mandal Yojna	
	Saraswati Sadhna Yojna	
	Vidhva Sahay	

(Table-3)

Visceral Design

One can find visceral design in advertising, folk art and crafts, and children's items. Children's toys, clothes, and furniture often reflect visceral principles: bright, highly saturated primary colors. These may not look like master art but they are enjoyable. The programs that are about the immediate, basic needs of the child and women have been designed with the principles of visceral design. This is where appearance matters and first impressions are formed that government wants their betterment. These are also generally programs of Central Government, part of Five Year Plans.

Balika Samruddhi Yojna

Balika Samruddhi Yojna was started with a view to bring change in the negative attitude of family and society towards girl child and mother, increase enrollment and attendance in the school, ensuring marriage at right age, providing financial aid to the girl child.

Under this scheme, two girl children from every household belonging to Below Poverty Level born on or after 15.08.1997 are covered for the benefits. **With a view of benefitting the girl child, the State government decided to continue the Balika Samruddhi Yojna even though the Central Government discontinued the scheme from the year 2006-07.**

Through this scheme, a benefit of Rs. 500 post-birth and while getting education, a sum of Rs. 300/- to Rs. 1,000/- scholarship upto 10th standard is added to their account as per the standards being passed. The Anganwadi (Kindergarten) workers provide aid to open savings account in any nationalized bank or post office. For the scheme, State expenditure is Rs. 10 crores for the year 2010-11, while there is a provision of Rs. 20.64 crore for the year 2011-12. During, 2011-12, a total of 24.93 lakh girls benefitted from the scheme.

Multipurpose Women Welfare Centers (MPWWCs)

MPWWCs numbering 261 have been formed across the state in 25 districts and 236 taluka and urban areas across Gujarat to help women deal with social, legal and employment related issues of women with the facility of help line. (Graph-II) MPWWCs have been provided with the audio visual kits to enable them in establishing dialogue with authority and experts through state satellite communication. The MPWCCs provide assistance to women under the Protection of Women against Domestic Violence Act, 2005.

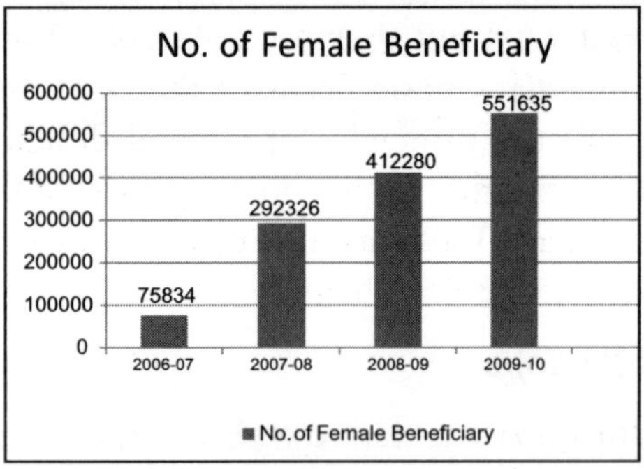

(Graph-II)

Swayamsidh Yojna

Swayamsidha is an integrated project for the development and empowerment of women. Swayamsiddha (swayam or self and siddha – the one who has proven capability or is empowered) project was introduced by Government of India during 2001 to 2002. The long term objective of the scheme is to achieve an all round empowerment of women – socio-economical-cultural empowerment by ensuring their direct access to, and control over resources through a sustained process of mobilization and convergence of all ongoing sector programs. The Women and Child Development Department of Gujarat implements the policy to help rural women be self reliant, gain confidence and learn the art of savings. It also focus on community oriented innovations, working in groups, building team spirit, mobilization of activities, gaining knowledge and awareness to empower financially. This project is envisaged in 20 regions at 26 spots covering 1760 villages which include 43,200 women and

2,700 initiating helpers. This project has brought women into the mainstream of development in the rural areas of Gujarat.

Behavioral Design

Behavioral level is about use, about experience with a program. In uses appearance doesn't matter much, rationale also doesn't matter but performance does and makes all the difference. But experience itself has many facets: function, performance, and usability. A program's function specifies what activities it supports, what it is meant to do – if the functions are inadequate or are not of interest, the program is of little value and, the program fails. Usability describes the ease with which the user of the product can understand how it works and how to get it to perform. If the person using the program gets confused and gets frustrated then it will lead to negative emotions. But if the program does what is needed, if it is comfortable to use and easy to satisfy goals with it, then the result is warm, positive effect.

Programs in this category are needed throughout the life cycle of a woman.

Fish Entrepreneur Yojna

Government encourages scheduled caste/tribe women to sell fishes to be self reliant. For the purpose, required instruments and facility is provided to buy weighing machine, insulated box, etc. On an average Rs. 10,000/- Unit cost, 50% assistance is given to women belonging to scheduled caste/tribe. Training is given to women for growth of 'zingo' fishes under a ten-day course with Rs. 100/- scholarship. (Annexure-3A & B)

Krishi Talim Yojna

Training in the field of Agriculture is imparted to women farmers and farmers' wives for research and use of latest technology. These women are paid stipend and given transportation to attend the training course.

Kunverbai nu Mameru Scheme

Government makes provisions for monetary help to persons belonging to scheduled caste families for their daughter's marriage under Kunverbai nu Mameru Scheme. Those who gets an annual income of Rs. 11,000/- can avail Rs. 5,000/- for their one daughter's marriage. For this, Rs. 2,000/- are given to girl's parents/guardian and Rs. 3,000/- is given to the girl in the form of Kisan Vikas Patra. (Annexure-4 A, B & C)

Mahila Vrudh Ashram

Aged parents neglected by youth is growing into order of the day. Therefore government has undertaken to make special arrangements for uncared women and foster their needs. State Government has set up old age homes for such destitute. Exclusive Women Old Age homes are structured with an exclusive existing home at Jamnagar.

Mid Day Meal

To ensure co-operation and enhance better quality of food with nutrition, the officials even share the food with children under 'Mid Day Meal' schemes which was started by the government as the second state in the country, committed to social integration and social upliftment.

Sakhi Mandal Yojna

The project aims to enable the poor women, particularly in rural areas of Gujarat, improve their access to resources and consequently strengthen livelihoods and quality of life. Sakhi Mandals are formation of women self help groups based on thrift and credit principles. (Graph-III). It provides financial services to accelerate the process of economic development and ensure welfare of women. They are encouraged to foster decision skills and develop a framework of wider range of participation in micro-finance development. (Annexure-5)

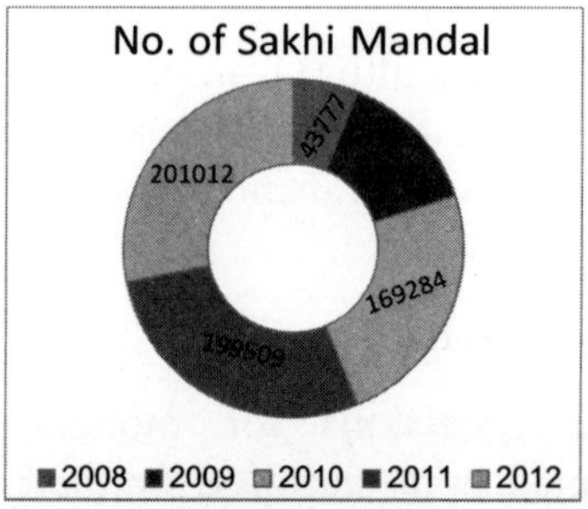

Growth in No. of Sakhi Mandals – (Graph-III)

Saat Phera Samuh Yojna

Joint marriages are more economical through government schemes in Gujarat. Minimum five couples and over, who get married and whose family income is upto Rs. 11,000/-, gets Rs. 5,000/- each in the form of Narmada Shreenidhi Certificate along with Merit Certificate. For organizing the Samuh Lagna, (group marriage), a sum of Rs. 1,000/- is offered.

Vidya Laxmi Bonds

Gujarat Government focus on role of Education in Poverty Eradication and the campaign is aimed at ensuring maximum enrollment of boys and girls in primary schools all across the state. To encourage Girl Child Education, Vidya Laxmi Bonds are entrusted among areas with low literacy rates, i.e. below 35 per cent among women, this serve as an incentive to poor parents to send their daughters to schools. (Annexure-6)

Vidyadeep Yojna

The state Govt. has introduced this scheme in memory of the students died in earthquake on 26th January, 2001. In Vidyadeep Yojna, the insurance covers the school going children and the premium is paid by the Government to provide financial relief to parents in case of accidental deaths. The scheme provides protection of round the clock insurance to the students studying in the government primary school, Grant-in-aid primary schools, ashram schools, secondary and higher secondary schools. Insurance cover is provided for Rs. 50,000/- .

In this scheme year 2010-11 total 85.00 lakh students were covered and 318 claims were made.

Vidya Sadhna Yojna and Saraswati Sadhna Yojna

Introduced first in Gujarat, this is an innovative 'Go Green' initiative. Provision of Rs. 1 crore has been made under Saraswati Sadhna Yojna to provide bicycles to Family Below Poverty Line (Vidya Sadhna Yojna) and Scheduled Castes students (Saraswati Sadhna Yojna) by the Gujarat Government. A sum of Rs. 1,500/- is provided to girls below 8th Grade to buy bicycle. Apart from this, provisions are made for students in elementary and high school education to get food and lodging, free of cost. (Annexure-7A & B)

Vidhva Sahay and Talim Yojna

Government is sensitive towards women of 18-40 years, who have lost their husbands and initiates policy for their empowerment and economic living condition. For their economic welfare, under Manav Garima Yojna, Rs. 3,000/- margin money is given to help them stand on their feet on their own and empower living. Women in the age group of 18-60 years are provided monetary help by way of application. The applicant gets Rs. 500/- and two children gets Rs. 80/- (per child) every month through post office. There is a group insurance scheme for widows for a cover of Rs. 1 lakh only. (Annexure-8)

Many Projects pertain to Urban Women like Savings and Investment Mandali (CDS-Samuhik Dhiran Mandali), Sports (8 lakh women participated in Khel Mahakumbh 2012-13, Annexure-9), Youth and cultural activities for women and children, Women and Children's Libraries, etc.

Reflective Level

Human nature enjoys to explore experiences far beyond the basic, biologically wired-in preferences. Thus, although bitter tastes are viscerally disliked (presumably because many poisons are bitter), adults have learned to eat and drink numerous bitter things, even to prefer them. This is an 'acquired taste,' so called because people have had to learn to overcome their natural inclination to dislike them.

Reflective level is where consciousness and the highest levels of feeling, emotions, and cognition reside. It is only here that the full impact of both thought and emotions are experienced. At the lower visceral and behavioral levels, there is only effect, but without interpretation or consciousness. Interpretation, understanding, and reasoning come from the reflective level. Of the three levels, the reflective one is the most vulnerable to variability through culture, experience, education, and individual differences. (Donald A. Norman)

Beti Bachhao and Nari Adalats are two examples of reflective level programs.

Beti Bachao

Gujarat has suffered gender based discrimination, i.e. declining male-female sex ratio. The state average of child sex ratio (0-6 years) declined dramatically from 928 in 1991 to 878 in 2001. To address this issue various efforts are being made, one of the major being the 'Beti Bachao Campaign' or 'Matru Vandana Yatra' that was launched by Chief Minister on the occasion of World Women's Day in 2005. Massive rallies are organized in all districts for community mobilization. College and high school students have been brought in to be active in the campaign by organizing essay writing and elocution contests in colleges and schools. The higher judiciary, lawyers of the state, District Development Officers and Collectors have been roped into the campaign through special conference.

In the city of Surat 1 million people took an oath to fight against sex discrimination and female feticide in 2007. Religious leaders also joined hands for a sustained impact.

The state regularly updates village wise data on sex ratio to monitor the situation.

Nari Adalat

The concept devised 'By women for women' – the Nari Adalats are operational for legal justice in over 34 regions (Table-4) in Gujarat. Women jurists dispense justice in women's cases of divorce, abandonment, violence, rape and dowry demands. These courts are set up for women empowerment and gender justice. These courts are not recognized by the State as a legal forum. However, the autonomous hybrid institutions are para legal authority who solve women cases faster than judicial courts. These courts are helping rural women overcome problems encountered in the normal judicial system. Inaccessibility, cost, time, unfamiliarity with legal procedures, inadequate resources, and a traditional disregard of the needs of women – all solutions get speedy, efficacy, and cost effective. The women leaders of the Nari Adalats use knowledge of local practices, customs, and social networks to gather evidence and negotiate agreements. They adjust meetings to the rhythms of life.

Regions	No. of Nari Adalats
Sabarkantha	5
Vadodara	7
Rajkot	11
Banaskantha	3
Panchmahal	5
Surendranagar	3
Dang	1
Total	**34**

(Table-4)

When assessing the extent of injustice to which the victim has been subjected, they retain their emphasis on ascertaining the rights of women within the framework of marriage, rather than outside it. Even as they generate social pressure on the offender – mostly the aggrieved woman's marital family and spouse – and quite often use the law enforcement system informally to intimidate a defiant violator, they acknowledge that maintaining the home and family is critical to their core understanding of gender justice. Their priority is to 'find a solution' for the woman within the ambit of social justice rather than applying more generic principles of judicial procedure or human rights. The Nari Adalats are thus a combination of indigenous norms based on a social understanding of women's rights and the statutory principles governing them.

The shared gender identity of the 'client' and the 'judge', the comfort of being in an environment which resembles your own extended family of mother, aunts, sisters and elders but which is more encouraging and emancipated, the non-intimidating space and the culture of communication without fear – all these elements of the Nari Adalats have a value which goes far beyond economic considerations for a woman who is battered and lost.

Women who come to the Nari Adalats want resolution more than justice. Their concerns are dominated by the practicalities of where they will stay, who will feed them and their children and the impact of their return to their parental home on their brother or on their sister's chances of getting married. Apart from a vindication of their rights, they require an urgent implementation of remedies and protection against the dominance of their marital home and the vulnerabilities of returning to their parental home or living alone. It has been found that there is also an implicit expectation by the aggrieved when approaching the Nari Adalat that they will receive a decision through this system which fits in with socially accepted norms, but that they will also be able to access the formal legal and judicial system with the support of the Nari Adalat, if necessary.

The popularity of the Nari Adalats also lies in the relatively high sense of control that the petitioner experiences there in comparison with the traditional panchs and the courts. Cost, time and venue are critical aspects in sponsoring a sense of control within the woman. The Nari Adalats, on average, take 3-8 months to resolve a case.

The process does not cost the petitioner much more than a thousand rupees - although this varies a little between Nari Adalats. From a one off fee of Rs. 100/-, to paying the travel and transport cost of the Nari Adalat members when they make visits to the petitioner's home for investigation, interrogation or counseling. One of the factors contributing to the client's sense of control is the fact that she can go to the Nari Adalat alone, without being accompanied by any member of her family (the traditional Panchayats would insist that she be accompanied by a male family member), or by a lawyer as would be the case in the formal system. In fact, the Nari Adalat places the client at the centre of the negotiations.

The experiences of some of Nari Adalat's clients after the outcome of their cases are enlightening, and provide critical feedback about alternate dispute resolution mechanisms such as these. There are no caste, class or religious hierarchies in the judicial process of the Nari Adalats. The Nari Adalats enjoy a high level of credibility within their own collectives, and in the blocks or talukas within their geographical regions.

Almost all clients the study team met were unanimous in their praise for the empowering way in which Nari Adalats had approached their issues, despite the fact that not all of them had received satisfying outcomes. (A Study of Nari Adalats and Caste Panchayats in Gujarat, Sushma Iyengar) (Annexure-10)

There is one other distinction among the levels: time. The visceral and behavioral levels are about "now," ones feelings and experiences while actually using the program. But the reflective level extends much longer—through reflection one remembers the past and contemplates the future. Reflective design, therefore, is about long term relations, about the feelings of satisfaction produced by being a part of the program. A person's self-identity is located within the reflective level, and here is where the interaction between the program and individual's identity is important as demonstrated in pride (or shame) of use.

The best kind of design isn't necessarily an object, a space, or a structure: it's a process - dynamic and adaptable. Till Gujarat Government didn't showed the way, constructed the framework for Women and Child Development, development programs for women had 'add women and stir' (Martin & Meyerson 1998) approach i.e. Simply deliver the same program to women that is delivered to men. This approach assumed that gender either does not matter or should not matter. Other approach was 'fix the women' (Ely & Meyerson 2000). This approach assumes that genders make a great deal but they locate the problem in women.

Gujarat Government not only designed but implemented the programs which neither victimized not blamed women but understood women as mother, wife, sister, and daughter, daughter-in-law and most importantly as an individual human being. The designs of programs of government of Gujarat are in harmony with the lifestyle of women. When something gives pleasure, when it becomes a part of our lives, and when the way we interact with it helps define our place in society and in the world, then we love that something, be it a product or a program. Love comes by being earned, when an object's special characteristics make it a daily part of our lives, when it deepens our satisfaction, whether because of its beauty, its behavior, or its reflective component. Design is part of this equation, but personal interaction is the key.

Narendra Modi by being part of all the programs himself has been part of personal interaction on behalf of government himself.

Designing Need Based Programs

The need, something which generally beneficiary finds it difficult to articulate can be fulfilled through enhancement or innovation. Enhancement means to take some existing program or service and make it better. Innovation provides a completely new way of doing something, or a completely new thing to do, something that was not possible before. Both are difficult to assess. Before the invention of television, personal computers, copying machines, cell phones, email or remote control, no one thought we need them.

Today it is hard to imagine life without these products, but before they existed almost no one but an inventor could imagine what purpose they would serve, and quite often the inventors were wrong. The personal computer was so misunderstood that several major computer manufacturers of the time completely dismissed them: some of those once-large companies no longer exist.

One cannot evaluate an innovation by asking potential users for their views. This requires people to imagine something they have no experience with. Their answers, historically, have been dangerously wrong. People have said they would really like some products that then failed in the marketplace. Similarly, they have said they were simply not interested in products that went on to become huge market successes. In India, as per a study, Hindi subtitles on songs in the song based program 'Rangoli' helped increase literacy. In far flung areas kids could identify the written words with the words that they heard in the song.

Predicting the popularity of a new product is almost impossible before the fact, even though it may seem obvious afterward.

Enhancements of a product comes from primarily by watching how people use what exists today, finding difficulties, and then rectifying them. Even here, however, it can be more difficult to determine the real needs than might seem obvious. People most of the time find it difficult to articulate their actual problems. Even if they are aware of a problem, they don't often think of it as a design issue. Best example of this is the issue of property ownership of the women, which was solved to great extent by simply waiving the registration fee if it is in the name of women or mobile anaganwadi for women working as labour.

How does one discover 'unarticulated needs'? Certainly not by asking, not by focus groups, not by surveys or questionnaires! Who would have thought of creating chocolate filled with nutrients for kids. It is only after such enhancements are made that everyone believes them to be obvious and necessary. Because most people are unaware of their true needs, discovering them requires careful observations in their natural environment. A person high on Spiritual Quotient, high on reflective thought can often spot difficulties and solutions that even the person experiencing them does not consciously recognize.

After function comes understanding. If one can't understand a product, one can't use it – at least not very well. Oh, sure, one could memorize the basic operating steps, but one probably will have to be reminded over and over again who he is. Similarly a program has to be designed in such a way that reinforcements are part of it. For this one needs to have different measure for human problems and the ability to move it through various programs.

In 1905 Alfred Binet and Theodore Simon developed the first modern intelligence test. These tests primarily measured intellectual or rational intelligence (used to solve logical problems). The higher the figure, the belief went, the greater the intelligence.

In mid-1990s, Daniel Goleman revealed findings in neuroscience and psychology that stressed the importance of Emotional Quotient (EQ). This makes us aware of our feelings and that of others. It gives empathy, motivation, compassion and an ability to respond skillfully to pleasure and pain. Goleman argued that EQ was a basic requirement for the use of Intelligent Quotient (IQ).

Dana Zohar and Ian Marshall introduced a new dimension to human intelligence: Spiritual Quotient (SQ). This is the intelligence used to solve problems of meaning and value. "Am I relating to the people in my life in a way that contributes to their happiness and mine?" Answers to these questions determine whether we will find happiness or not. IQ and EQ are inadequate in such issues.

Spiritual Quotient is defined as, "The intelligence with which we address and solve problems of meaning and value, the intelligence with which we can place our actions and our lives in a wider, richer, meaning-giving context, the intelligence with which we can assess that one course of action or one life-path that is more meaningful than any other." Spiritual Quotient essentially integrates Intelligence Quotient and Emotional Quotient. It is our ultimate intelligence.

Some of the programs are listed below (Table-5) as per their quotient.

IQ	EQ	SQ
Kishori Shakti Yojna	Mamta Abhiyan	ICDS

(Table-5)

IQ is associated with the *serial processing activity* of the brain (rational thought). It is associated with our neural tracts. Neural tracts learn (are wired) according to a fixed program, the rules of which are laid down in formal logic. The learning involved is step-by-step and rule bound. When we teach children their time-table by rote, we are encouraging them to wire their brains for serial processing. It produces the kind of thinking that is useful for solving rational problems or achieving definite tasks.

Kishori Shakti Yojna and NPAG

In the year 2000, the Ministry of Women and Child Development, Government of India, came up with a scheme called Kishori Shakti Yojna (KSY), which was implemented using the infrastructure of the ICDS. The objectives of this scheme was to improve the nutrition and health status of girls in the age group of 11 to 18 years, to equip them to improve and upgrade their home-based and vocational skills, and to promote their overall development, including awareness about their health, personal hygiene, nutrition and family welfare and management.

Thereafter, the Nutrition Programme for Adolescent Girls (NPAG) was initiated as pilot project in the year 2002-03 in 51 identified districts across the country to address the problem of under-nutrition among adolescent girls. Under this programme, 6 kg of free food grain per beneficiary per month was given to the undernourished adolescent girls.

Government of India provides Rs. 1.10 lakh per project for implementation of KSY. For 2011-12 and 2012-13, there was a budgetary provision of Rs. 222.20 crores under KSY being operational in 17 districts of Gujarat. A total of 5,72,059 adolescent girls were enrolled under KSY. Under the Kishori Shakti Yojna, the Government of India was providing Rs. 1,10,000/- per block annually. However, no separate budget for supplementary nutrition was given. As a State Initiative, in 2005, State Government initiated giving supplementary nutrition to 10 adolescent girls per Anganwadi center which was later extended to 20 adolescent girls per AWCs since 2010-11. As per March 2012, total of 4,80,850 Adolescent girls received supplementary nutrition.

Scheme for Empowerment of Adolescent Girls (SABLA): A comprehensive scheme called Rajiv Gandhi Scheme for Empowerment of Adolescent Girls (RGSEAG) has been launched by the Government of India to address the multi-dimensional problems of adolescent girls. The KSY and NPAG schemes have been merged into this. SABLA has been implemented initially in selected 200 districts across the country, using the platform of ICDS. In these districts, RGSEAG has replaced the KSY and NPAG schemes. In the remaining districts, KSY would continue as before. The scheme has 2 major components:

- Nutrition component: wherein energy dense food is being provided at the AWC. The beneficiaries would be 11-14 years out of school adolescent girls and all girls in the age group of 15-18 years.
- Non-nutrition component: Here, the focus would be on out of school girls only.

Emotional Quotient: Associative thinking underlies most of our purely emotional intelligence (EQ) – the link between emotions and bodily feelings, emotions and the environment. It is also able to recognize patterns like faces or smells, and to learn bodily skills like riding a bicycle or driving a car. It is 'thinking' with the heart and the body and so is thought of as our 'emotional intelligence' or the 'body's intelligence'. The structures within the brain with which we do our associative thinking are known as neural networks. Unlike the precise wiring of *neural tracts (Intelligence Quotient)*, in neural networks each neuron acts upon or is acted upon by many others simultaneously.

Unlike serial neural tracts which are rule bound or program-bound and thus unable to learn, neural networks have the ability to rewire themselves in dialogue with experience. All associative learning is done by trial and error. This kind of learning is experience-based: the more times one performs a skill successfully, the more inclined he will be to do it that way the next time. Associative learning is also tacit learning – One learns the skill, but he can't articulate any rules by which he learned it and usually can't even describe how he did so. Neural networks are neither connected with language faculty, nor with the ability to articulate concepts. They are simply imbedded in experience. One feels his skills, he does his skills, but he doesn't think or talk about them. One develops his skills because they give one a sense of satisfaction or a feeling of reward,. or because they help him avoid pain.

Thus most emotions are developed by trial-and-error, a slow associative build-up of response to certain stimuli and they are quite habit-bound. Once one has learned to feel anger at a given situation, it is difficult for the individual to react differently next time.

It is more flexible but less accurate than serial thinking. The disadvantages of this type of thinking are that it is slowly learned, inaccurate and tends to be habit-bound or tradition bound. We can relearn a skill or an emotional response, but it takes time and much effort. And because associative thinking is tacit, we often have difficulty sharing it with others. We can't just write out a formula and tell someone else to get on with the job. *All of us must learn a skill in our own way, for ourselves.* No two brains have the same set of neural connections. (Daniel Goleman)

Mamta Abhiyan

MAMTA stands for 'Malnutrition Assessment and Monitoring to Act'.

MAMTA also means Mothers Love.

Mamta Abhiyan, a joint four-pronged health and nutrition service delivery strategy has been initiated by the State of Gujarat in early 2007. The four components include:

1. Mamta Divas (Village Health and Nutrition Day)
2. Mamta Mulakat (Post Natal Care Home Visit)
3. Mamta Sandarbh (Referral and Services)
4. Mamta Nondh (Record and Reports)

Purpose

- To promote and provide preventive health and nutrition services at village level
- To operationalize service with convergence among health and ICDS departments

Goal

- To enhance reach, access, and utilization of the integrated health and nutrition services

The components of Mamta Abhiyan are:

Mamta Day (Health and Nutrition Day):

This is a monthly fixed day fixed site joint nutrition and health delivery strategy implemented in each village. Along with routine immunization, services such as micronutrient supplementation (IFA, Calcium, Vitamin A and iodine through free 1.5 kg of iodized salt for all pregnant and lactating mothers), Hemoglobin test for the pregnant woman at the time of registration and also in the 6th and the 8th month, urine testing of pregnant woman for albumin and sugar with Uristix and counseling are provided by health and Anganwadi workers. Additionally growth monitoring for children under-three ever quarter is carried out by health/ICDS supervisors. On the first contact, the pregnant mother receives a Mamta Card which she carries along with her on all subsequent Mamta Days. This card is not only a record of services received by her but also includes pictorial messages on healthy maternal and childcare behaviours. Hence, it also serves as a counseling tool which is used by workers to counsel the mothers during Mamta day as well a reminder which can be referred to by mothers at home.

"I wish the Mamta Divas Abhiyan was there when I had my first child. She is 13 years old and looks eight or nine. My son is a different story," says Meenaben Gavit, proudly holding her one year old son on her lap. "I had three antenatal checkups when I was pregnant with him, got all my supplements and immunization. My son was born in a hospital. The Auxiliary Nurse and Midwife (ANM) made three postnatal visits within the first 10 days of his birth. He got his BCG shot on Mamta Divas and his immunization is up to date all because of Mamta Divas" (Innovation, Unicef, 2009)

Positive Development

In Gujarat, angan wadi workers of every test checked angan wadi center were trained for analysis of growth chart.

Growth charts in all test checked angan wadi centers were maintained by the angan wadi workers.

Chapter 6, Supplementary Nutrition, Report no. 22 of 2012-13-Union Government (Ministry of W&CD) Report of the CAG on Performance Audit of ICDS Scheme

Mamta Sandarbh (Referral Services) – One *Mamta* Referral Centre has been developed in each block. Services of a pediatrician who has been commissioned on call basis are available on a definite day (Thursday) at the Referral Centre to provide medical care to the children found with acute and chronic illnesses, through screening on Mamta day.

Mamta Mulakaat (Postnatal Home Visit) – Three postnatal visits are conducted by the ICDS/Health worker on Days 1, 3 and 7 after birth of the child. Mothers are supplemented with postnatal vitamin A (2 lakh I.U.) on the first visit and provided counseling on child care and exclusive breastfeeding in all visits.

Mamta Nondh (Records and Reports) – are records/reports of all above-mentioned activities. Using these reports, data is compiled and block-wise data is used to review and identify poor performing blocks.

In brief, Mamta Abhiyan is a comprehensive package of preventive, promotive, curative and referral services under the Reproductive and Child Health Programme (RCH II) initiated in 2006.

The association with mother and child is also kept alive through various other initiatives like:

Annaprashan Day

Annaprashan is a fixed day, fixed time, fixed site monthly counseling strategy for symbolic and timely initiation of complementary feeding. Annaprashan Diwas is celebrated on every fourth Friday between 12 noon to 2 pm at every Aanganwadi center. The main target audience for this program is care givers of infants 6-9 months of age. On the day of Annaprashan Diwas, the mothers of children 6-9 months of age and mothers of severely underweight children gather at the AWCs. They are counseled on optimal feeding practices like continuation of breastfeeding along with complementary feeding upto 2 years, hygienic feeding practices, appropriate feeding for children during and after illness etc. For young children symbolic initiation of complementary feeding is done.

World Breastfeeding Week Celebrations

World Breastfeeding Week is celebrated from 1-7 August every year across the State. Awareness generation activities like mothers' meetings, meetings of pregnant women, lactating women and adolescent girls are held to orient them about the importance and benefits of breastfeeding. Health workers, AWWs, AWHs facilitate these meetings.

National Nutrition Week Celebrations

The National Nutrition Week is celebrated from 1-7 September every year across the State. Activities like recipe competition, demonstration of nutritious recipes, mothers' meetings, importance of nutritious diet for pregnant and lactating women etc. are carried out during this week. Mothers are counseled on complementary foods to be given to children, importance of IFA tablets to improve hemoglobin, need and benefit of iodized salt, foods rich in iron and other nutrients etc.

Doodh Sanjeevani Yojna

The ICDS is carrying out the 'Doodh Sanjeevani Yojna' in collaboration with the Tribal department. Under this scheme, double fortified milk (100 ml) is provided to each child twice a week. The budget allowance is Rs. 2.45 per beneficiary for 1 time supply of 100 ml milk. This scheme is implemented with the help of local dairies.

Mamta Taruni

Mamta Taruni day is a joint DWCD & DHFW initiative which was launched State-wide for out of school adolescent girls, 10-19 years delivered monthly on Mamta day (VHND) between 3-5 p.m. Even before initiation of SABLA: Gujarat already has initiated a scheme for Adolescent girls – 'Mamta Taruni day' from April 2010.

Package includes: Bi yearly Hb estimation

- IFA tablets
- TT at 10 and 16 years
- Quarterly: Weight and Height
- ICDS Take Home Ration (3 packets of Upma, 2 packets of Sheera, 1 packet Sukhadi)
- Referral to Adolescent Friendly Health Centre
- Delivered by ANM, AWW, ASHA and Peer Educator (which a leader Adolescent girl selected 1 per village)
- A compensation of Rs. 50/- Anganwadi Worker and Rs. 25/- Peer Educator is given provided atleast 10 Adolescent girls receive the benefits and services.

In the year 2006-07, Government of Gujarat initiated provision of supplementary nutrition to 10 out of school adolescent girls per AWC across the State. Looking at the increasing demand, the number of adolescent girls was increased to 20 per AWC in 2009-10. Gujarat is the first state in the country to carry out this initiative. In March 2010, 336,410 adolescent girls were provided supplementary nutrition, while in February 2011, the number increased to 7,46,445 girls. The entire expenditure is borne by the State Government.

SQ is our conscience. It is what makes us essentially human: the ability to plan, to make sense of our emotions, to control our impulses, to make choices, and endow our world with meaning. The frontal lobes of the brain are where our ideas are created; plans constructed; thoughts joined with their associations to form new memories; and fleeting perceptions held in mind until they are dispatched to long-term memory or oblivion. (Daniel Goleman)

This brain region is the home of consciousness. Self-awareness arises here, and emotions are transformed in this place from physical survival systems to subjective feelings. This is frontal lobe, that Rishis have traditionally placed as Third Eye – the gateway to the highest point of awareness. Through this one can feel the wants of needy. Narendra Modi has the ability to not only feel but also fulfill the same. This is reflected in following initiatives.

ICDS scheme is a central government scheme implemented across country. But Gujarat has a distinct place in its implementation. As an attempt towards addressing the issue of maternal and child under nutrition, ICDS has undertaken various initiatives at state and district level besides the schemes and efforts of Government of India. ICDS in Gujarat

Positive Development

In all test checked anganwadi centers of Gujarat 80 gm RTE energy foods were introduced as part of RDA.

In Gujarat green leafy vegetables, other vegetables, seasonal fruits, milk and egg were incorporated in the supplementary nutrition in the entire test checked anganwadi centers.

Chapter 6, Supplementary Nutrition, Report no. 22 of 2012-13-Union Government (Ministry of W&CD) – Report of the CAG on Performance Audit of ICDS Scheme

The revised norms effective from February 2009, inter alia, included serving of more than one meal to the children of the age group three to six years at the angan wadi centers that included morning snacks and hot cooked food since children of this age group might not be able to consume 500 calories in one sitting. Further ready to eat micronutrient fortified food was mainly provided to the beneficiaries in place of hot cooked food. The children only in the age group of six to three years were to be provided supplementary nutrition in the form of Take home ration.

Test check revealed that the revised norms were implemented only in the Gujarat.

Chapter 6, Supplementary Nutrition, Report no. 22 of 2012-13-Union Government (Ministry of W&CD) – Report of the CAG on Performance Audit of ICDS Scheme

presently covers over 51.48 lakhs beneficiaries (children under 6 years, pregnant women, lactating mothers and adolescent girls) through 50,225 operational Anganwadi centers (as on March, 2012).

State Government of Gujarat contributes additionally to the ICDS implementation in addition to Central Government's support.

Supplementary Nutrition Program (SNP)

Supplementary Nutrition is provided at the Anganwadi Centers in the State as per the Government of India guidelines. But in most of the areas Government of Gujarat has enhanced the Government of India's initiatives. The details are as under:

- Energy Dense Micronutrient Fortified Extruded Blended Food (Bal Bhog) is provided as Take Home Ration (THR) to children 6 months to 3 years (7 packets per month, i.e. 3.5 kg) and underweight children 3-6 years (4 packets per month i.e. 2 kg) on Mamta Diwas. Each packet weighs 500 gms. The shelf life of these premixes is 4 months. It can be easily prepared by mixing it with hot milk or water.
- Energy Dense Micronutrient Fortified Extruded Blended Take Home Ration (THR) like Sukhadi (1 packet of 1 kg per month), Sheera (3 packets of 500 gm each) and Upma (2 packets of 500 gm each) are provided to pregnant women, nursing mothers and adolescent girls.
- Freshly cooked afternoon meal prepared from wheat flour is provided to the children (3-6 years) coming at the Anganwadi centers.
- Hot cooked breakfast is provided through Matru Mandals and Sakhi Mandals in 18,543 AWCs covering 12,60,610 children in the age group of 3-6 years (March, 2012).
- Matru Mandals and Sakhi Mandals are involved in the Supplementary Nutrition Programme to promote community participation and to maintain the quality of food Currently, 7.2 lakhs beneficiaries (pregnant women, lactating mothers and adolescent girls) from 9,591 AWCs are being covered through

these Mandals. They prepare the supplementary food and provide to the beneficiaries at the AWCs twice a week.

- Additionally, the State Government is also providing fruits (seasonal) as morning breakfast to children 3-6 years, twice a week (Monday and Thursday) at the AWCs.
- The State has also initiated 'Doodh Sanjeevani Yojna' in selected 10 Blocks of 6 Tribal districts, wherein, 100 ml fortified, flavoured, double toned pasteurized milk is provided to children 3-6 years, twice a week. During 2010-11, around 1.77 lakhs children were benefited from this scheme from 784 AWCs while in the year 2011-12, around 44,557 children were benefitted from this scheme from 1,519 AWCs. This initiative is being implemented with the help of local dairies.
- Nutri-Candy with micronutrients and vitamins (Iron – 7 mg, Vitamin A – 300 IU, Ascorbic Acid – 10 mg, Folic Acid – 15 mcg) is given to children in the age group of 3 to 6 years in addition to regular food supplement in Anganwadis is another first by the state of Gujarat. Nutri-candy has a weight of 3 grams and is processed by a manufacturing unit and procured and supplied through Gujarat State Civil Supply Corporation.
- Milk and Sukhadi through community support – As per the instructions by the Chief Minister, a special effort to promote community participation has been started since June 2008. The community has been involved to provide Milk and Sukhadi to the ICDS beneficiaries (children) during the School Admission Drive and Anganwadi Admission Drive. During 2011-12, Rs. 17.92 lakhs were collected through community participation and 1,64,403 pregnant and lactating mothers and adolescent girls were provided with 'Sukhadi'.
- Tithi Bhojan – Through this initiative, the community provides various foods like fruits, sweets, snacks etc. to the children at AWCs on several occasions like birthdays, marriage, religious ceremonies, fair etc.

During 2011-12, for Supplementary Nutrition, there was a total budgetary provision of Rs. 637.94 crores of which state share was Rs. 407.04 crores and that of central govt. was Rs. 230.90 crores. Thus, the state spent an additional of Rs. 176.14 crores from state budget on ICDS over an above the normal CSS norms.

The beneficiaries under SNP have already been universalized in the state. Thus all categories of children (6 months to 6 years) irrespective of their caste/tribal status etc. are being covered under the program.

The cost sharing ratio between centre and states with regards to SNP as effective from the year 2009-10 is given below (Table-6). Here also state government's contribution is higher than central government.

Cost Sharing Between GoI and GoG for Supplementary Nutrition

S. No.	Beneficiaries	Financial Provision by GoI in Rs.	Actual Expenditure in Rs.	GoI share in Rs. per Beneficiary	State share in Rs. per Beneficiary
1	6-36 months Normal Children	4.00	5.29	2.00	3.29
2	6-36 months Severely underweight Children	6.00	7.93	3.00	4.93
3	3-6 years Normal Children	4.00	4.34	2.00	2.34
4	3-6 years Severely underweight Children	6.00	6.98	3.00	3.98
5	Pregnant women, Lactating mothers, Adolescent girls	5.00	6.65	2.50	4.15

(Table-6)

Following table mentions the State expenditure incurred in 2011-12 (Table-7 & 8).

Type of Beneficiaries	Number of Beneficiaries	Actual Expenditure per beneficiary per day in Rs.	Estimated total expenditure as per current norms for 3 days of Nutrition in Rs.
6 months – 3 years Normal Children	15,80,887.00	5.29	2,50,88,67,669.00
6 months – 3 years Severely Underweight Children	48,728.00	7.93	11,59,23,912.00
3-6 years Normal Children	12,74,384.00	5.48	2,09,50,87,296.00
3-6 years Severely Underweight Children	39,255.00	8.13	9,57,42,945.00
Pregnant Women	3,87,904.00	6.65	77,38,68,480.00
Lactating Women	3,43,219.00	6.65	68,47,21,905.00
Adolescent Girls	10,65,282.00	6.65	2,12,52,37,590.00
Total	**47,39,659.00**		**8,39,94,49,797.00**

(Table-7)

100% State Burden:

1	Fruit	15,76,00,000.00
2	Nutri-Candy	9,06,00,000.00
3	Milk – Dudh Sanjivni in 10 Block of Tribal Area	1,66,00,000.00
		26,48,00,000.00

(Table-8)

In sum Gujarat State Government is incurring an additional expenditure to the tune of Rs. 212 crores on providing extra nutritional benefits from the state budget to all target beneficiaries i.e. all 6 months to 3 years children, adolescent girls and pregnant and lactating mothers in order to combat the problem of high prevailing under nutrition among children and for emphasized focus on improving the nutritional status of women and children.

Quality Control Mechanism

Regular testing of various food samples is done for the food given under Government of Gujarat's scheme. The random samples collected from the field are sent to the NABL labs every month for testing by the State Commissionerate Office. From June, 2010 approximately 450 samples have been sent for testing till, June, 2012 for laboratory testing for microbiological parameters.

Additionally, teams of ICDS – PO and CDPOs have been sent to districts / blocks for field monitoring for supervision of the supply chain management of the THR etc.

Own Buildings of AWCs

Anganwadi Centers (AWCs) are the basic infrastructure identified and developed in every target village for delivery of the services and deliverables to target beneficiaries of the ICDS program.

In the last four years, the State Government has provided Rs. 350 crores towards construction of 10,960 AWCs from State budget. In the year 2010-11, the unit cost of AWC was raised from Rs. 3 lakhs to Rs. 3.23 lakhs with a provision of Rs. 100 crores to construct 3,095 AWCs as per the new rate. For the year 2011-12, there was a provision of Rs. 100 crores for AWC construction. Similarly, in the year 2011-12, the unit cost of AWC was raised from Rs. 3 lakhs to Rs. 3.94 lakhs with a provision of Rs. 100 crores to construct 3,095 AWCs as per the new rate. For the year 2012-13, there is a provision of Rs. 511.91 crores for AWC construction. A provision of Rs. 511.91 crore is made for construction of 12,045 new anganwadi Nandghars during 2012-13 of which 7,832 are sanctioned in rural and 4,213 in urban municipalities.

What is evident from the following innovation and its success of the ICDS program is that SQ replaces the ego with the soul, both as the seat of personal identity, and as the governor of IQ and EQ. SQ therefore exercises IQ and EQ from the soul, instead of from the ego. Only when soul comes into action then one can think of reaching out to every single individual however far he or she may be and provide him or her with the same comfort which others are enjoying. When IQ (thought) and EQ (emotion) are governed by SQ (spirit), thoughts and emotions are transformed in quality and given a whole new purpose. This helps in taking the programs to next level e.g.

Mobile Anganwadi Centers

The State Government has provided vans for Mobile Anganwadi Centers to address the needs of the socially excluded population, mostly residing in the interior areas of the State. The State has 46 Mobile Anganwadi Vans for improving coverage of the eligible beneficiaries.

Honorarium to Anganwadi Worker

Besides the honorarium being given by Government of India, additionally Rs. 500 for AWW and Rs. 250 for AWH is being spent from the State budget. Further, in Swarnim Siddhi year 2010-11, State Government again increased the honorarium of AWW and AWH on 01-05-2010 wherein there was an increase of Rs. 500 per month for AWW and Rs. 250 for AWH, (Table-9). For this, State Government is incurring an extra expenditure of Rs. 95 crores during 2010-11. For the financial year 2011-12, there is a provision of Rs. 95.97 crores for this purpose.

	Existing Honorarium effective from 1-04-08 per month	Increment by GoI 01-04-11	Increment by State Government			Total per month
			01-10-07	01-05-10	01-05-12	
AWW	Rs. 1500	Rs. 1500	Rs. 500	Rs. 500	Rs. 250	Rs. 4250
AWH	Rs. 750	Rs. 750	Rs. 250	Rs. 250	Rs. 100	Rs. 2100
AWW of Mini AWCs	Rs. 750	Rs. 750	–	Rs. 250	–	Rs. 1750

(Table-9)

The State Government has initiated several welfare measures for the AWWs and AWHs, the details of which are given below:

Human beings are more than IQ. Success, satisfaction and happiness are not purely a function of intellect. A whole and happy human being is made up of a combination of factors that go way beyond intellect. There is a need of self actualization even at the lowest level of worker. Gujarat Government understands this and takes steps towards fulfillment of such needs.

Mata Yashoda Award for Best Performing AWW and AWH

State Government has implemented motivational awards for Anganwadi Workers, who can be easily called the backbone of Women and Child Development program.

> **Positive Development**
>
> In 2007-08, Gujarat Government introduced Mata Yashoda Award to one angan wadi worker and angan wadi helpers comprising Rs. 51,000 and Rs. 31,000 respectively as a state level award.
>
> *Chapter 5, Human Resource and Training Report no. 22 of 2012-13-Union Government (Ministry of W&CD) – Report of the CAG on Performance Audit of ICDS Scheme*

The award was named Mata Yashoda Award by the Chief Minister Narendra Modi himself. He says that its Mata Yashoda who groomed Lord Krishna when his parents were jailed by Kansa. Such a deep thought in naming a program or award can come only from a person who has a very high level of spiritual quotient.

With an objective of strengthening the ICDS services and to motivate and acknowledge the exemplary work of AWWs and AWHs, Mata Yashoda Awards are being given by State Government at State, District, Municipal Corporation and Project levels from 2006-07. From year 2007-08, the best performing AWWs and AWHs are given Mata Yashoda Award by Chief Minister on 8th March every year. (Graph-IV)

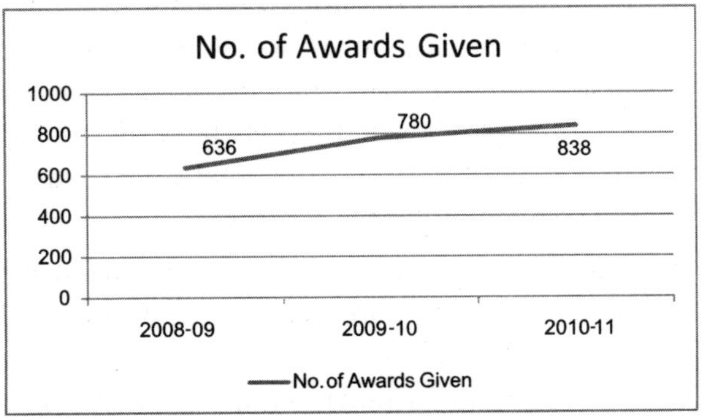

Mata Yashoda Award (Graph-IV)

During the year 2011-12, an expenditure of Rs. 3.8 crores was incurred for provision of awards. Following are the details (Table-10):

Level of Awards	**Anganwadi Worker**	**Anganwadi Helper**
State Level Awards	Rs. 51,000	Rs. 31,000
District Level Award	Rs. 31,000	Rs. 21,000
District Level Award for Municipal Corporation / Maha Nagarpalika	Rs. 31,000	Rs. 21,000
Project Level Award	Rs. 21,000	Rs. 11,000
Project Level award for Municipal Corporation / Maha Nagarpalika	Rs. 21,000	Rs. 11,000
Nagarpalika / Corporation level Award	Rs. 21,000	Rs. 11,000

(Table-10)

Mata Yashoda Gaurav Nidhi – Insurance Scheme for AWW and AWH

In an attempt to provide social security to AWWs and AWHs, Mata Yashoda Gaurav Nidhi Insurance Scheme is being given by Gujarat State Government in collaboration with Life Insurance Corporation. **Gujarat is the first State in the country to provide an insurance coverage for AWWs and AWHs.** Under this scheme, every month a premium of Rs. 100 is paid out of which Rs. 50 is paid by Gujarat Government and Rs. 50 is paid by the beneficiary (AWW/AWH). Out of the total amount of Rs. 100, Rs. 17 is paid towards premium of the scheme and the remaining Rs. 83 is kept as savings on which interest is received by LIC. On maturity of the insurance, the nominee of the insured receives an amount of Rs. 50,000 in case of death of the insured and the interest of the money being deposited. During 2010-11, a total 77,825 AWWs and AWHs have been covered under the scheme whereas during 2011-12, a total of 94,308 AWWs and AWHs have been covered under the scheme.

An expenditure of Rs. 5 crore has been incurred by the State Government for year 2010-11 and there is a provision of Rs. 5 crore each for the year 2011-12 and 2012-13. In case of death or retirement, assistance is given in Mata Yashoda Gaurav Nidhi Yojna. So far the assistance been given has been detailed in Table-11 below:

Cause of Assistance	No. of Cases	Expenditure in Rs.
Death	206	1,03,00,000.00
Retirement	2574	44,46,031.00
Total	2780	1,47,46,031.00

(Table-11)

Grading of Anganwadi Centers

The Department of ICDS has initiated the process of grading the Anganwadi Centers (AWCs) on the basis of their performance to ensure quality service provision at the centers. The criteria for grading the AWCs are (Table-12) below:

• Availability of basic amenities at AWC • Actual attendance of children against those enrolled for pre-school education • Provision of pre-school education • Enrolled Beneficiaries receiving supplementary nutrition • Health services • Mamta Day celebration	• Use of growth charts and community chart • Status of malnutrition • Community participation • Gender awareness • Home visits • Record maintenance • Other activities • Observance of various schemes like Kishori Shakti Yojna, Balika Samriddhi Yojna etc.

(Table-12)

Providing 2 Saree and Blouse to All AWW and AWH Every Year

In order to acknowledge, appreciate and give a separate identification to AWWs and AWHs, Gujarat Government in the year 2008-09, initiated giving two sets of saree and blouse along with stitching charges to all Anganwadi Workers (AWWs) and Anganwadi Helpers (AWHs). In the year 2008-09, the saree and blouse sets were distributed to 88,358 AWWs and AWHs for which the state incurred an expenditure of Rs. 5 crore. There is a provision of Rs. 7.59 crore in the year 2011-12. These sarees have been designed by National Institute of Fashion Technology (NIFT), Gandhinagar.

After seeing the Gujarat State initiative, Central Government started giving a grant of Rs. 200 per saree and blouse set.

Badge to AWWs and AWHs

Badges have been given to all AWWs and AWHs – to give them identity in the village and also as motivation.

Money, saree can fulfill the basic needs of an individual but for motivation one needs respect. By providing as small a thing as a badge, Chief Minister of Gujarat has been successful in fulfilling the needs of self actualization, in its employees at the ground, across the state which is evident from the success of the program.

If SQ is not active, IQ and EQ are used by the ego to seek personal compensations for the dissatisfaction of being the ego. But when SQ is active, IQ and EQ are used for a different purpose. SQ uses IQ and EQ to share the qualities of the soul for the benefit of all. This leads one to think of programs cutting across departments as well as public-private partnership.

The Women & Child Development Department is collaborating with various line departments to provide effective services to the community. The details of the inter-sectoral convergence are as below:

Departments of Health and Food & Civil Supplies

The ICDS collaborates with Departments of Health and Food & Civil Supplies for the provision of iodized salt at the AWCs on Mamta Diwas, free of cost, to pregnant and lactating mothers. The indent of requirement is prepared by the ICDS and handed over to the Department of Food & Civil Supplies. The financial support for this is provided by the Department of Health.

Tribal Development Department

The ICDS is carrying out the 'Doodh Sanjeevani Yojna' in collaboration with the Tribal department.

Total Sanitation Campaign (TSC) and Water Supply Department

The Total Sanitation Campaign (TSC) programme of GoI concentrates on providing toilets to all households, schools and Anganwadi Centers. Under this programme, District Rural Development Agency at the District level receives a proposal from ICDS regarding the village wise requirement of toilets. The requirement is then included in the annual implementation plan of the district.

> **Positive Development**
>
> In Gujarat drinking water was available at all angan wadi centers.
>
> *Chapter 5, Human Resource and Training Report no. 22 of 2012-13-Union Government (Ministry of W&CD) - Report of the CAG on Performance Audit of ICDS Scheme*

Based on the requirement district funds allocated under TSC for AWCs are transferred to ICDS for implementation/construction of the toilets.

Water and Sanitation Management Organization (WASMO) is a registered autonomous body under Bombay Charitable Trust Act by Government of Gujarat. This organization primarily facilitates provision of drinking water facility in villages and AWCs through 'Paani Samiti' constituted under gram panchayat. Anganwadi centers are also covered under this programme for making the toilets functional.

Food & Civil Supplies Department

The department provides wheat (whole) – 65 gm per child per day and fortified oil (5 g) at the AWCs.

> **Good Practices in Gujarat**
>
> State Government provided gas stoves, LPG cylinders and idli cookers at cost of Rs. 33.10 crore to its 49,926 anganwadi centers.
>
> From 2009-10 onwards State Government pays Rs. 200 per anganwadi center towards the electricity bill.
>
> *Chapter 4, Infrastructure Development Human Resource and Training Report no. 22 of 2012-13-Union Government (Ministry of W&CD) - Report of the CAG on Performance Audit of ICDS Scheme*

Nutri-candy is supplied by the Food & Civil Supplies Department. The grant for this is provided by ICDS. Nutri-candy has a weight of 3 grams and is processed by a manufacturing unit and procured and supplied through Gujarat State Civil Supply Corporation.

Department of Rural Development

Sakhi Mandal scheme is effectively implemented by the Department of Women and Child Development in convergence with the Department of Rural Development.

Government of Gujarat runs various stages of the programs under Public Private Partnership.

a) Construction of Anganwadi Centers

Gujarat Government visions that every Anganwadi center should have their own fully equipped buildings. Anganwadi centers are built through Public Private Partnership (PPP). For example, companies like Reliance, Syntex, Atul Industries, Adani Group etc, as part of their Corporate Social Responsibility (CSR) initiatives, are providing financial support in building Anganwadi centers in some villages, while the space for construction of Anganwadi Centers has been provided by schools, Panchayati Raj Institutions (PRI) etc. in many other villages.

b) Gas Connections at Anganwadi Centers

The Government of Gujarat is providing gas connection along with gas stove and cooker to all the Anganwadi centers across the state. For this, the Department of ICDS has collaborated with State Government Public Sector Units under the Corporate Social & Environmental Responsibility (CSER) and about Rs. 33.43 crores have been spent since 2010 to provide Gas connections in all AWCs with 2 gas bottles, gas stoves and cooker.

When IQ and EQ are governed not by the ego but by the soul, one experiences and creates a different world. SQ therefore represents the necessary and sufficient means of individual and collective transformation.

Case Study: Need & Want Based Program

Integrated Child Development Services (ICDS) was launched in Gujarat in the year 1975 in the Chhota Udepur Block of Baroda District under the aegis of State Health Department and was functional under Health Department till 2003. Since 2003 it is functional under independent department – 'Women and Child Development Department'. Over the year, new blocks were added under the ICDS program and along with this the coverage of health services like immunization also have improved. But activities like growth monitoring, nutrition education, referral services and supplementary nutrition invariably lagged behind. This was largely due to:

- Uncoordinated expansion under Health Department and ICDS Scheme, such as between the growth of Primary Health Centers (PHCs), Sub-Centers (SCs) vis a vis ICDS blocks with more Anganwadi workers and sector supervisors.
- Over a period new districts and blocks were created by the State Government and jurisdiction area under each office changed.

Government of Gujarat recognized the interrelated (Diagram A), activity of both the departments and took corrective measures.

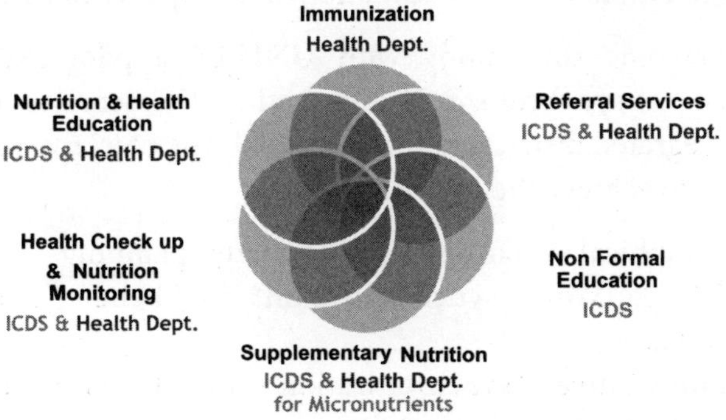

Diagram A: Interrelated Nature of Activities Between Health and ICDS

In the year 2007 Government of Gujarat, Department of Health & Family Welfare and Department of Women & Child Development jointly initiated Mamta Abhiyan which covered all aspects of services provided under ICDS and Health Services. Mamta Abhiyan is a joint four-pronged health and nutrition service delivery strategy. (Diagram B).

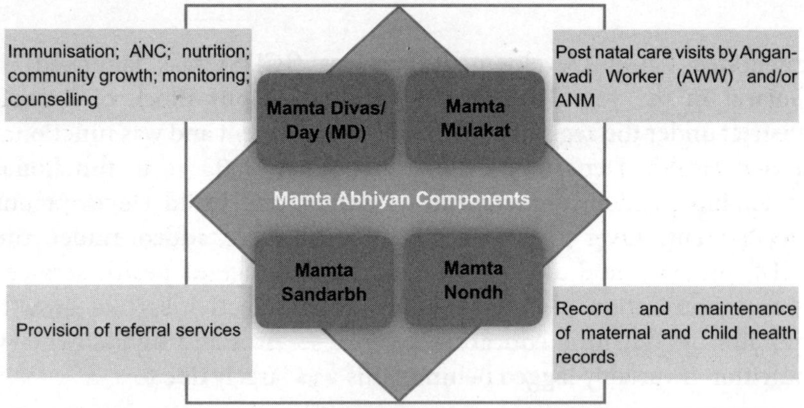

Diagram B

This program threw up some new challenges, like:

- Completely different jurisdictions of health and ICDS supervisors.
- Some areas overlapped while many were left uncovered.
- Different work schedules and calendar of activities at all levels.
- Overall difficulty in coordination, joint supervision and synergy.

To overcome this, along with UNICEF a pilot exercise was undertaken to synchronize Health and ICDS services in Valsad district (integrated district) in the year 2007. The objective of this pilot project was to achieve the following:

- Geographical synchronization for better planning.
- Functional/Work synchronization, for better joint service delivery.
- Administrative synchronization of better supervision, monitoring and accountability.

Geographical Synchronization

In each block, there were four Primary Health Centers (PHCs) (Diagram C) and 13 ICDS sectors. One PHC catered to a population of about 30,000 while One ICDS supervisory area catered to a population of about 15,000-16,000 (15 Anganwadi centers). (Diagram D) Some ICDS supervisory sector fell under the jurisdiction of different PHCs e.g. sector 2, 4, 9, and 10, making it difficult for the ICDS Supervisor to jointly plan and review the health and nutrition services with the health staff of two different PHCs.

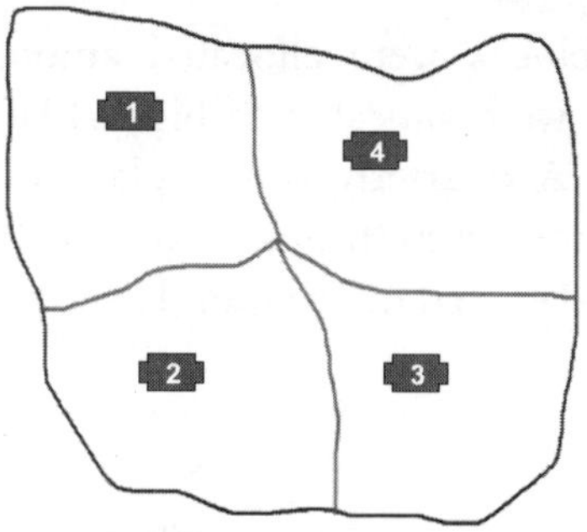

Diagram C: Geographical Boundary of PHCs in a Block

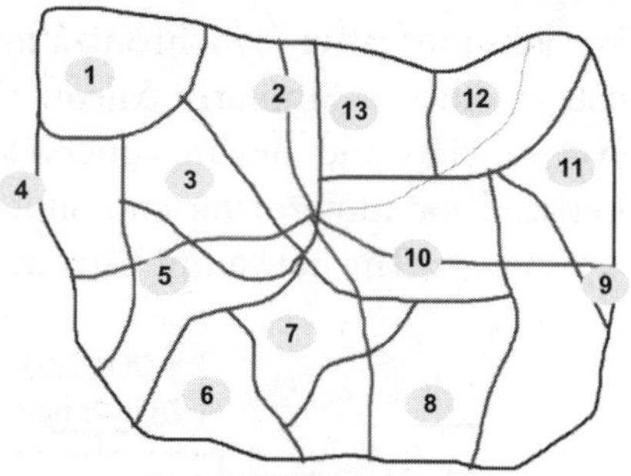

Diagram D: Geographical Boundary of ICDS Supervisory Sectors in a Block

For achieving geographical synchronization, a task force consisting of Health and ICDS officials was formed at district level. As per their recommendation, geographical areas were redistributed. (Diagram E). This resulted in improved coordination and better planning, supervision and monitoring as well.

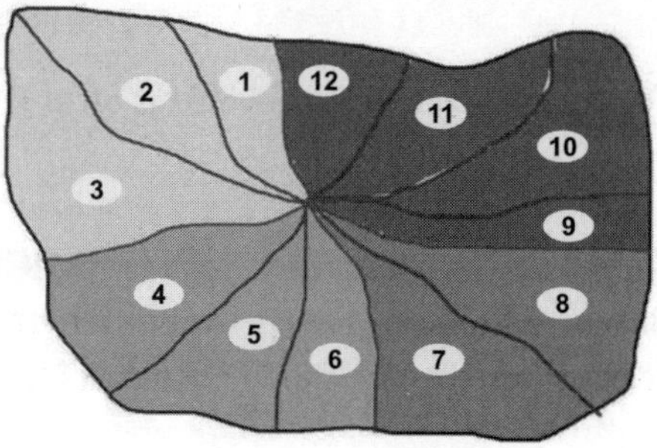

Diagram E: PHCs and ICDS Sectors After Synchronization

Functional Synchronization for Joint Service Delivery

A fixed monthly plan was prepared by Medical officer of the PHC for every 1,500 population, which was approved by the Block Health Officer for every village. Quarterly activity plan were worked out for monitoring, providing counseling and other curative services.

More than 2,000 Health and ICDS functionaries were oriented on the need for working together as a team to deliver both Health and ICDS services from and under the same roof.

Administrative Synchronization for Review Meeting

For administrative synchronization, blocks were allocated among district officers. Similarly Anganwadis were allocated to block/PHC level officials and health supervisors. A quarterly action plan was prepared for monitoring and supervision by both health and ICDS Supervisors. The new administrative is depicted in Diagram F.

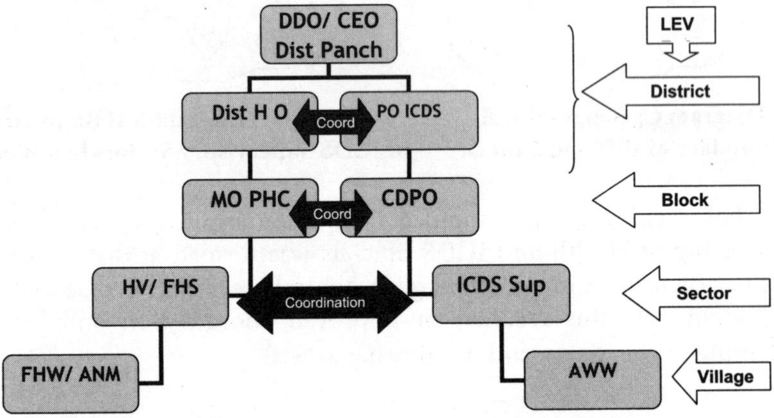

Diagram F: Administrative Synchronization at Different Levels

Results

Multi Indicator Cluster Evaluation Survey (MICES) conducted in Valsad in 2008 clearly showed an improvement in nutrition behaviours and service access compared to 2007 (Diagram G).

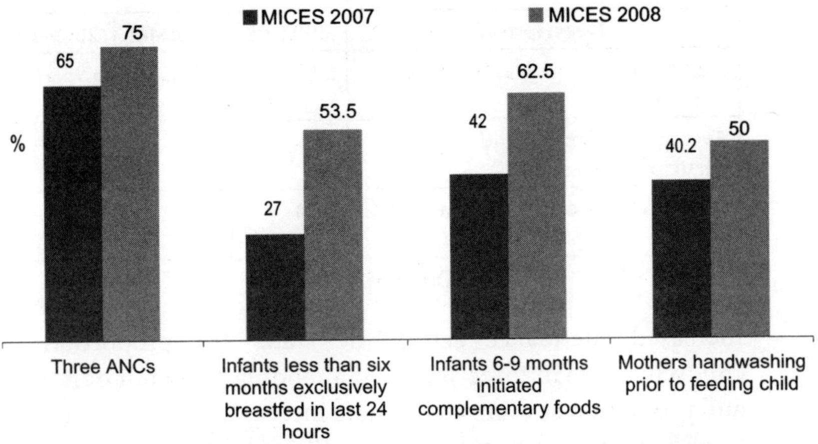

Diagram G: Effect of Synchronization on Key Indicators in Valsad District

> **Positive Findings**
>
> In Gujarat 100 per cent anaganwadi centers had functional baby weighing machines.
>
> *Chapter 4, Infrastructure Development Human Resource and Training Report no. 22 of 2012-13-Union Government (Ministry of W&CD) – Report of the CAG on Performance Audit of ICDS Scheme*

Subsequently, these results were shared with the government and a decision was taken to replicate the strategy across the state. Five regional conventions of Health and ICDS Managers were held to orient them regarding the synchronization process for successful implementation in their districts. Visits were organized for Health and ICDS officials to observe benefits of the synchronization exercise in Valsad. Synchronization exercise was replicated in the entire state by the end of 2008. These initiatives had a long term positive effects.

- Across the state of Gujarat, Mamta Day sessions registered a 50% increase from 2007-08 to 2009-10, with an average of 33000 Mamta Day sessions taking place each month across the state. On an average 1.5 Million (64%) of less than three years old children in rural Gujarat are being weighed every month. (Table-13)

Description	2007-08	2008-09	2009-10
Number of Mamta Day Sessions organized	2,62,353	3,17,496	3,93.312
Average number of child participants/session	16	37	44
% of mothers covered by three ANC visits	69.4	73.4	76.2

(Table-13)

- Increased attendance across the state: The proportion of children less than three years old attending growth monitoring and promotion sessions in the state increased from 25% in 2006 to 65% in 2009; equating to 1.5 million children attending per month.
- Increase in regular attendance and willingness to seek advice: Women attend Mamta day regularly and are more willing to consult Female Health Workers when their child is unwell. This is demonstrated by children with diarrhea in the last two weeks who have received oral Rehydration Salt increasing from 33% in 2003-04 to 39% in 2007-08. IMNCI performance reporting indicates an increase in childhood illness being managed better at the community level.
- Increase in antenatal checkups: The percentage of women receiving three antenatal checkups increased from 65% in 2007 to 84% in 2010.
- Increased in exclusive breastfeeding: Exclusive breastfeeding (until six years) increased from 27% to 61% between 2007 and 2010.
- Increase in complementary feeding: Initiation of complementary feeding by seven months increased from 42% to 72% from 2007 to 2010.

The Synchronization exercise that was carried out by the Government of Gujarat was a tedious process. It not only involved administrative orders and government resolutions but working together at various levels across the state. This demands, mindset change, getting together non-homogenous groups/departments, patience/tact to handle resilient fellows/political un-will and close monitoring for trouble shooting.

Not only this, functional synchronization at all levels is an ongoing activity and requires regular motivation and facilitation at all levels. It was successful is best reflected by the fact that this initiatives resulted in inclusion of a basket of other services on Mamta day such as iodized salt, postnatal VA mega dose, Calcium tablets to pregnant women, out-of school adolescents, community growth monitoring etc.

Apart from the benefit to the masses, this program turned out to be beneficial for the government also. It created a 'we can work together' feeling, which stimulated collective thinking resulting in related line departments to work together to achieve common goals.

It doesn't surprises one when in Chapter 3, Universalization of ICDS Scheme, Infrastructure Development Human Resource and Training Report no. 22 of 2012-13-Union Government (Ministry of W&CD) – Report of the CAG on Performance Audit of ICDS Scheme one finds the following:

"Out of 7015 sanctioned ICDS projects, 6722 projects were operationalised. The maximum shortfall in operationalisation of projects occurred in Delhi (42 per cent), and West Bengal (28 per cent)" while Gujarat has a success rate of 100 per cent.

The data from annexure 3.1 of the above report is represented in the Graph-V below:

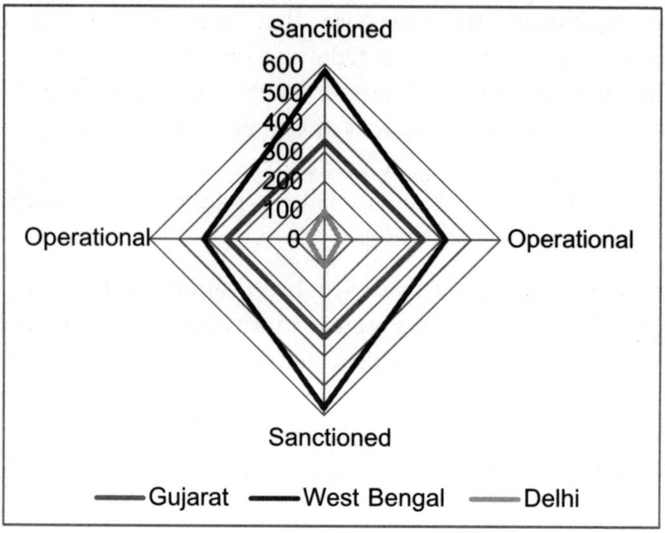

Graph-V : Sanctioned Vs Operational ICDS Centers

ICDS program clearly reflects the importance of SQ in governance and Visceral Design in program designing. Whereas IQ is rule based, EQ helps us act appropriately within prescribed boundaries, SQ helps extend and change the boundaries, question set assumptions and formulate new meaning. "My own research indicates that it is inextricably linked with creating order (less entropy) in the brain from chaos (high entropy). Bringing about new order in our brain is facilitated by engaging in activities related to our least conscious part of the brain (our creative mode) in a playful, non-dutiful fashion. SQ is our compass 'at the edge.'" (Zohar & Marshall 2001, pp. 13-14):

Spiritual Quotient is developed primarily through reflection. Consider thinking. Thinking is not just a generic term for the collection of skills housed in the brain. It involves many of them: recollection and imagining in particular. But it includes something that is not part of any other function: self-awareness. This aspect of thinking is captured in the word often used to describe it: reflecting. (Carter 1998, p. 191)

Chief Minister Narendra Modi has demonstrated what reflective thinking can achieve.

Judgment

Rest assured this will be a day (Shala Praveshotsav) that no child will forget during his entire life!

– Narendra Modi

On the second day of the three-day long Praveshotsav in 2009, Narendra Modi, taught poet Botadkar's poem 'Janani ni jod sakhi nahi jade re lol' to students of the primary school in Jhamp village in Sanand taluka. He not only recited the poem but explained the essence of poem and of the word 'Maa'. Judgment is the essential genome of leadership. And a political leader is judged by others on the performance of his or her government. Government's performance is reliant on many factors; e.g. who to put in key jobs, how to manage a program introduction or policy change. Each of these performance factors whether big or small requires judgment.

From 14th June to 16th June 2012, in the rural areas 34,000 government primary schools were covered in a three day initiative of Shala Praveshotsav and Kanya Kelavani (Annexure-11) in 18,000 villages of Gujarat. 4,79,808 children including 2,34,302 girls and 2,45,506 boys in the age group below five years enrolled in schools. New enrolled children were given school bags, slate-pen, books, notebooks, pencils, uniform etc. without any cost incurred by the beneficiary. Also 74,466 girls were given Narmada bonds worth Rs. 14,89,32,000. Individuals and different organizations contributed Rs. 10.53 crore to Kanya Kelavani Nidhi in 3 days. On similar lines, the program happened from 28th to 30th June 2012 in urban areas, covering primary schools in 6 Mahanagarpalikas and 159 Nagar Palikas.

As per the Census-2011 data, there were 4.19 crores literates in the state with nearly 1.8 crores literate women. The last decade saw an increase of 59.60 lakh female literates in the state. Gujarat witnessed a phenomenal jump of 12.93% decadal increase in female literacy, overtaking states like Tamil Nadu, Maharashtra, Karnataka, Andhra Pradesh, Madhya Pradesh and Rajasthan. The significant increase in number of literate women and female literacy rate has been witnessed in both rural and urban areas of Gujarat.

There is a distinction between judgment and decision making. Judgment is a process that unfolds over time. A leader's success hinges on how well he/she manages the entire process, not just the single moment when a decision is made. Tichy and Bennis in their book 'Judgment' write that a leader should have a teachable point of view. Teachable point of view is an articulation of the idea that helps organization be successful, the values required to be on the team, and how one will energize people along the way. Ideas, Values and Emotional Energy become the guidepost for making judgments. (Figure-1)

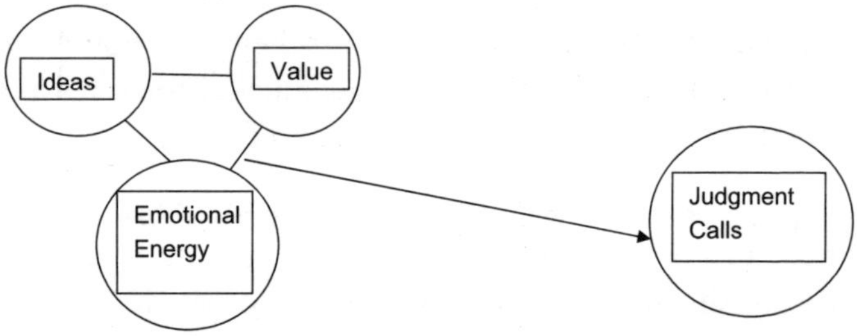

(Figure-1) Jeff Immelt's Teachable Point of View Shapes Judgment Calls

Ideas

Chief Minister Narendra Modi donates all the gifts that he receives to Kanya Kelavani Nidhi.

Great organisations are built on central ideas. By passing ideas to others and teaching others how to develop good ideas, leaders create organizations that are finely tuned towards delivering success. The ideas provide the answer to: Where are we going? What are we aiming to accomplish? (The Cycle of Leadership)

The Educated Girl Child Initiative was born out of a painful distress call as Women's Education in Gujarat in 2001 stood on 20th Position with Literacy rate among female with 48.1%. This programme came out of the realization that social factors are responsible for rural population not sending their children to school. Praveshotsav is a massive annual awareness drive in which during the admission season in June every year, the entire bureaucracy which includes officers of all departments of the government go to each and every primary school and village to solicit the parents to send their children to school for studying. This programme was started in the year 2003 and has been successfully continued till date.

Radhika Srivastava (UNICEF, 2005), in her article 'In Gujarat, Niloshi's five-year olds enroll in school amidst jubilation' wrote the following: "A broken mountain road ascends to Niloshi village in Valsad district of Gujarat, one of the relatively prosperous states of India. Niloshi, located at a rugged end of the Western Ghat mountains, is home to one of the most backward tribes in the state.

However, on June 17, Niloshi woke up to a joyful occasion involving all households. All five-year olds in the village were to be enrolled in the village primary school on that day. Niloshi, with a female literacy rate of 6.5 per cent, was determined to bring about a radical change. Parents who had never been to school were dancing and singing as they saw their little ones go to school.

'The drum-beaters whipped up a frenzy with their music and accompanying them were wind instrument players. Coloured paper flags stuck to a string hung on bamboo poles along the road. At the centre of all the activity were about thirty children, all below six years who stood in a line outside the village temple, waiting to be enrolled in school. All wore paper crowns and were clearly very pleased with all the attention they were getting. Their small hands reached out every now and then to adjust the diadems on their heads.

To chaperone them were about a hundred older children wearing their light blue school uniform, holding placards that read 'Tell us a story', 'Be kind to us', 'Do not beat us', 'Do not scold us' – messages the new students were conveying to their teachers. The older students took the younger lot to school in a lively procession through the village. "I am feeling very proud of my girl who will now go to school. I am glad I decided to enroll her. I will let her study as much as she wants," said Kanta Dhakal, mother of five-and-a half-year-old Sarika.

Next to Sarika stood five-year old Manisha, daughter of Navsu Bhoya, an illiterate farmer who remarked, "Had the Shala Praveshotsav not been held, I would not have known that it was time for Manisha to join school. I always thought she was too small and could wait for a couple of more years."

Balubhai Ganga Bhai Pawar, the village headman, who has played a key role in leading the drive and motivating parents said, "We sent out messengers to all homes to speak to parents of children not yet enrolled. This is how the villagers came to know of the event and agreed to send their children to school. Our preparations include training by UNICEF in which we learnt how to make crowns and placards."

Positive Development

In Gujarat all the eligible children joined the formal education.

Chapter 7, Pre-school Education, Human Resource and Training Report no. 22 of 2012-13-Union Government (Ministry of W&CD) – Report of the CAG on Performance Audit of ICDS Scheme

The School Enrollment Drive, an annual event, aims to reach all children above the age of five and getting them enrolled in primary schools. Between June 16 and 18, this drive was held in all 18,618 villages in Gujarat. As a result 235,085 children (118,728 boys and 116,357 girls) were enrolled. The initiative began after Gujarat was shown to rank 21st among the 35 States and Union Territories in India in terms of its literacy status, especially that of girls and women. A large number of teachers have been recruited in the past couple of years and several scholarship schemes have been started for children in villages. The enrolment drive is part of the effort to put all children in school. The state chief minister, Narendra Modi, launched the campaign by pleading with people to get their girls admitted to school.

In the crowd Sat Sankadi, a tribal woman and her son Jamu, 5, who has six elder siblings, none of whom goes to school. "I came to know through my neighbour about the Shala Praveshotsav. So I have brought my son here," she said. "For many generations, nobody in my family ever went to school. Our children would help us with cattle grazing. But I think Jamu should get a chance to study," she said.

Sankadi was not quite sure how education would help Jamu lead a better life, but she was willing to give it a try. "I have heard that education is necessary. And I have hope that at least Jamu might benefit from it," she said.

Values

We need Saraswati more than Lakshmi now, although we are chasing the latter more.

– Narendra Modi

Winning leaders articulate explicitly and shape values that support development ideas. The values element guide the organization in the kinds of behavior required to be a member of the organization. (The Cycle of Leadership)

Values behind Kanya Kelavani and Shala Praveshotsav program are:

a) To make the people aware of importance of girl child education.

b) To have 100% enrolment of children in Standard 1.

c) To reduce the dropout rate particularly of female child by creating awareness about importance of their continuation in school.

d) To give bureaucracy a firsthand exposure of problems of education at the primary level in villages and in cities / in rural and in urban areas.

e) To get first hand feedback from the people of the village about quality of education, quality of mid day meal, teachers' absenteeism, infrastructure in education, etc.

f) To make teachers conscious of the fact that some high level official visits them every year and thus giving them an opportunity to showcase whatever good work they may have done.

"I travel all the way from Ahmedabad to teach children. It gives me immense satisfaction to see the government actively taking part in it and providing all these facilities," says Priyanka Chauvan, a teacher at the primary school in Siyawada.

Emotional Strategy

When the individual strength latent within the women is successfully transformed into the community's strength, then only can real social enlightenment happen.

– Narendra Modi

Winning leaders have a clear set of beliefs and actions for motivating others to buy into and internalize the values of the organization. Winning leaders are also motivated and they motivate others about change and transitions. Leaders energies others when they personally interact with them. (The Cycle of Leadership)

The Kanya Kelavani Praveshotsav came out of the vision of the Chief Minister Narendra Modi. All the Class II and above officers, numbering about 3,000, plus all the ministers, MLAs and MPs, office bearers of district and taluka panchayat, cover atleast 15 villages within a period of three days every year at the time of admission in June. Accordingly, routes are chalked out for visit of each officer to a set of 15 villages which are close to each other. Every year in the month of June, on pre-decided dates, Kanya Kelavani and School Admission Drive is organized at the village level. It covers almost 18,000 villages on this day, young children are gathered in a bullock cart and taken to school. A common briefing cum training session is held every year before this program by use of satellite media, in which officials visiting schools are briefed thoroughly about what they are expected to do when they go to a village. This briefing meet is the main important element of this program. From 2003 to 2011 for last 9 years, each of these briefing meet is also addressed by Chief Minister himself in order to motivate officers to do this job as a pious duty rather than ritual. In the drive, all IAS, IFS and IPS officers are also involved. For some of those officers, who have never worked in the field of education, this kind of exposure coming year after year, is found to be personally very enriching for them.

Analysis of the Judgment of Kanya Kelavani Praveshotsav

Good judgment further the story, bad judgments disrupt and hinder the story.

The strategy of social awareness which was created because of Kanya Kelavani Praveshotsav worked very well. Infrastructure in primary school was never lacking, what was lacking was social awareness about importance of girl child education among certain castes and tribes. This issue was addressed by focusing attention of the entire bureaucracy, by sending them to each and every school every year in the meeting with the village people. Also this program is one of the most favorable programme of Chief Minister Narendra Modi. When the emphasis of some aspect of social change comes from the top, the whole machinery is galvanized.

Census figures stand as an independent testimony of the fruits of this program. The change in literacy rate, particularly in female literacy rate, being more than 40% more as compared to the previous decade, itself shows that this effort of promoting girl literacy has paid off. (Graph-VI & VII)

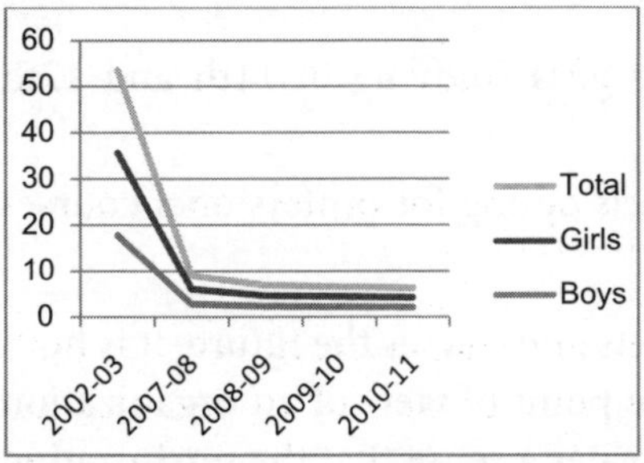

Graph-VI: Standard 1 to 5

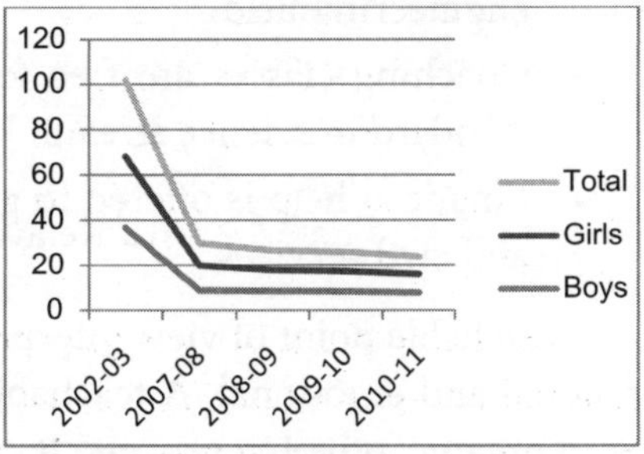

Graph-VII: Standard 1 to 7

A prima facie inference is that a large proportion of children born after 2001 are becoming literate.

During the Kanya Kelavani and School Admission Drive, activities like mothers' meetings, decoration of home and AWCs, recipe competition, recipe demonstration etc. are conducted. All the children enrolled in the school are provided with Vidya Laxmi Bond, school bag and kit. Four-year old Pooja is all smiles. She has just received a school bag, a pack of books and chocolates at the primary school in Jaakhaura.

The children from AWCs enter into the school with blessing from the local leaders. Those children not going to school are also enrolled and re-admitted to the school, to prevent dropouts.

District wise Kanya Kelavani Gaurav Puraskar to institutions or individuals is furthering the cause of girls education.

This year (2012), Girls who live 3 km or more from their schools were given bicycles – around 48,000 new cycles were distributed across the state. Takht Singh Chauvan used to worry about his daughter Sarita. "I had to drop her to school which was about 3 km away. This resulted in delay for work," said Takht Singh. Today both the father and daughter are happy. Sarita has just received a bicycle from the state government and she is excited to come to school riding it.

Some of the other initiatives aiming many to promote girls education are:

- Computers are given to girls studying in medical and engineering field.
- Coaching classes are free for girls studying in 11th and 12th standard in science stream.
- Financial help is offered to girls opting for professional courses and civil services.

Teachable point of view interprets and shapes the future. It is both rational and emotional. A teachable point of view of an organization is an organic, ongoing process. It creates a sense that the organization is embarked on an ongoing journey. It defines the beliefs, attitudes and values that the organization holds and that its employees share. It comes from the hearts and engages people emotionally and personally. Chief Minister of Gujarat shares its teachable points of view through Karmyogi Abhiyan. Karmayogi Abhiyan is a campaign launched by Narendra Modi to transform the Kamacharis into Karmayogis by imparting training to over a five lakh employees of the State Government. This has never been thought of by any other Government in India.

Karmayogi Abhiyan harnesses the strength of Government employees and has sensitized them as accountable public servants. Training includes working skills, pranayam and yoga. Karmayogi Abhiyan is not only to enhance professional skills amongst officers and employees but also to enrich their personal life.

Chintan Shibirs are annual 3-day programme for all ministers and senior officers for discussion, progress review and goal setting for the next year. Through these chintan shibirs, collectors and DDOs are provided a platform here to share the best practices that could be replicated elsewhere in the country. Collector and DDO are also given awards for their performance. Gujarat Government allows the bureaucracy to dream, experiment and realize focus on solutions. In the 7th edition of the annual Chintan Shibir – 2011, 'Main Nahi, Hum' (say no to I, say We), said Chief Minister Narendra Modi addressing the gathering. The brainstorming session saw the Chief Minister leading from the front inspiring officials to see the role of public service in a holistic light. He wins over bureaucrat's heart by conveying the importance of their role in upliftment of Women and Child in the state of Gujarat. Money is very small component in the factors required to motivate and enthuse a bureaucrat. There are districts in Gujarat where malnourished children are under direct supervision of districts government officials. These steps have been taken voluntarily by bureaucrats. This ownership comes from the realization that their actions make a difference and sensing that they are valuable member of the team. Chief Minister Narendra Modi through his teachable point of view creates a feeling that "we are all in this together, and we will succeed or fail, based on the actions of each person." (The Cycle of Leadership) This was also visible when PHC centers were reorganized to synchronize with ICDS centers. Judgment is a complex process and it unfolds in several dimensions. Chief Minister Narendra Modi has mastered it.

Third Curve

"Till now we were only able to exploit 50% of our manpower in economic development. Now through these Shakti Mandals the remaining 50% of the women power would also be activated and channelized for the development of Gujarat and India. This is my dream of Inclusive development."

– Narendra Modi

Anandiben Patel, Gujarat's Minister of Revenue, Roads and Buildings, Capital Project, Women and Child Welfare in an interview answering to the question: There was no women and child development ministry in Gujarat till 2001. What led to having a separate ministry? said: "Women make up for 50% of the social force. Children make up for another 25%. Inclusive growth could not be achieved by neglecting such a huge chunk of the population. A special machinery was needed to look after the socio-economic-educational welfare of women and children. Shri Narendra Modi was sensitive to the issue, and hence the welcome change."

From the formation of Women and Child Development Ministry in 2001 to Mission Mangalam in 2010, Gujarat has taken an unbeatable lead in women and child development in India.

Gujarat's existing women and child development systems, structures, processes and culture can be termed to as the 'Third Curve' of the development sector.

From the perspective of development science, development designs in the 'First Curve' of development have origin in the initial steps of industrial designs. Most of the states' women and child development program, including Government of India's program fall under First Curve. First Curve developments are essentially Five Year Plans. Unfortunately Five Year Plans more often become the objective of vote bank politics. This plan objective drift transforms the saner objective itself into sloganeering, failing to deliver development and its intended goals. (Most of the time, if not always)

Today, women and child development systems in India are on the 'Second Curve' paradigm of development only in the states of Chhattisgarh and Madhya Pradesh. 'Second Curve' is a more evolved set of system, organizational and process designs that are required to satisfy the increasing wants of beneficiary in the knowledge economy. Both the states achievements are remarkable considering one is infested with naxal issues and the other has a long history of neglect of women and child development by previous governments. These Second Curve states are engaged in redesigning their core systems and processes. In rest of the Indian States 'The Second Curve' is yet to emerge and unfold.

What is this Shift from the First to Second to Third Curve?

The critical distinction between the first and second curve is that the first curve is focused much more on making products or services. The first curve is dependent on money. It is where capital is important. It is a production oriented phenomenon; whereas the second curve nearly always has a sort of passionate and deep understanding of consumer wants. It is more about people. It is incredibly dependent on the capacities of individual human beings rather than simply on financial dimensions. Simply having money doesn't mean one can build a second curve. One can't do it without people and the right kind of people. While, Third Curve (Graph-VIII) is about satisfying needs, and it needs high spiritual quotient.

Third Curve needs leaders. Albert Einstein suggested that we cannot create solutions for today's problems if we remain embedded in the original thinking that generated them. He was talking about paradigms. For example,

On the occasion of International Women's Day, over 400 women from 160 coastal villages of Gujarat attended a seminar by the Gujarat Ecology Commission on constructive use of Solar Energy for sea farming. The participants were taught practical skills like using solar energy equipment for fish drying and crab fattening that can contribute to the value addition of their marine products.

Connect between Solar Energy and Women in India, doesn't goes beyond, 'lighting of homes & streets' and 'cooking food'. It has component of first curve, like Government of Gujarat provides subsidy to fisher women to buy fishery related equipments under Fish Entrepreneur Yojna, but paradigm shift happens when the needs are satisfied. In case of Gujarat, paradigm shift is visible not only in application of solar energy but almost in all the State Government sponsored programs.

James Ogilvy says, "Fresh thinking about the future calls for alternative scenario based on new assumptions that differ from the old, not just quantitatively but qualitatively. A coherent set of qualitatively new assumptions amounts to a new paradigm, a new way of looking at something we thought we knew." Chief Minister Narendra Modi designs new ways of doing things. He mixes talents, skill and interests, leading to paradigm shift.

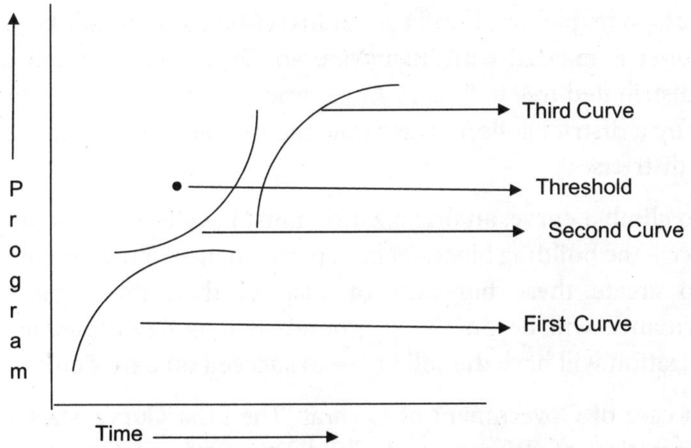

Graph-VIII : Third Curve of Women and Child Development

First Curve assumptions and beliefs about how to organize Women and Child Development delivery are deeply embedded in Five Year Plans. Since Independence, women and children development model and rigid bureaucratic service delivery systems are besieged with their industrial age organizational practices and have been delivering miniscule incremental change.

In Third Curve change differs from incremental change, in that it requires new ways of thinking and behaving. Third Curve change is path breaking in scope, not discontinuous but a major shift from the past and irreversible. Incremental changes in Second Curve development system are limited by scope and reversible taking care of the fear that just in case the change doesn't work out.

The Third Curve cannot be achieved until and unless the delivery system and the organizational component parts are intentionally designed with entirely new paradigms. Political Leadership and Bureaucratic Leadership's satisfaction and a desire on their part 'to be part of the team' and 'to do better' are part of Third Curve. One of the examples of the bureaucrats taking up in designing new program is of 'Bhagwan No Bhag'.

In the program 'Bhagwan No Bhag' i.e. 'God's Share'; every milk man who comes to sale his milk at the milk cooperative center, donates, pours part of his milk as per his wish in a container kept there. Container is marked with 'Bhagwan No Bhag'. The milk collected is then distributed free to kids in Anganwadi centers. This initiative was taken by a district collector and now the model is being replicated in other districts.

To climb a curve, an organization must have the right foundation in place – the building blocks of high performance. If the organizations fail to create these bulwarks of success, then the organizations performance will be on shaky ground. If it is developed properly, organization will have the solid base to succeed on a new curve.

In case of Government of Gujarat 'The First Curve' started with the formation of 'Women and Child Development Department' in 2001. But what is more important is that the process of Second Curve had begun along with the formation of First Curve. Committed to improve the condition of women of the state, the Government of Gujarat initiated the formulation of the State Gender Equity Policy in line of the National Policy for Women's Empowerment, 2001. This policy aimed at integrating gender perspective in all the existing as well as the new programs/schemes that would be implemented by the state government.

Following were the objectives of this policy:

- To incorporate gender perspective into various government programs.
- To enact new laws and providing legal services to women in distress.
- Capacity building of both genders in order to bring about attitudinal changes along with skill development.
- To view health and education as the focal themes of this policy.
- Ensure linkages between various development programs/ schemes related women, under different government departments.
- Better coordination between government and non-government organisations.

The first meeting for the State Gender Equity Policy was held under the Chairmanship of Anandiben Patel, Minister for Women & Child Development, Government of Gujarat. It was decided to form nine different groups for the formulation of the policy, focusing the key issues related to women. A chairperson was nominated for each group comprising experts from different fields such as NGOs, Researchers, Academicians, Government Departments, implementers etc. It was also decided to appoint a Consultant for each group who would guide the group members and raise key issues of concern. The members were nominated for each group who are experts in the respective field. All the members were requested to participate in the task of policy formulation.

Eventually, the draft policy documents submitted by the consultants were compiled into one compact policy document highlighting the policy prescription, action points and agencies responsible for the actions for each thrust area represented by various groups. This document was widely circulated among all the participants in the policy formulation process and other experts in the field for their suggestions and comments.

A State Level workshop was held which was attended by the Minister for state for the Women and Child Department Anandiben

Patel, the group members including the Chairpersons and Consultants and other expert invitees. In the workshop, the consultants carried out a brief presentation of the issues raised and remedies suggested by the groups during the policy formulation meetings. Each presentation was followed by a panel discussion. The suggestions and comments resulting from the workshop were incorporated and the policy was finalized by the Department of Women and Child Development.

The State sanctioned and announced the state policy for Gender Equity as 'Nari Gaurav Niti'.

Nari Gaurav – dignity and respect for a woman's life, her work, her concerns, her rights is central to the development of any society. A woman in the role of mother, wife, daughter, daughter-in-law has been responsible for bearing the burden of the unpaid care economy by contributing immensely to human resource development which in turn contributes to the economic development of a society. The question is do we recognize the unequivocal contribution of a woman towards development of society and her rights to benefit from the society? The response is that the Government of Gujarat does.

Nari Gaurav Niti, the State Policy for Gender Equity, was announced by Government of Gujarat in 2006 for the development and empowerment of women in the state is based on Mahatma Gandhi's principles on women's rights and equality. The guiding philosophy of the policy is that women and men have equal rights, opportunities and responsibilities to contribute to the well being of the society. The approach of the policy is to promote gender equity and equality by putting gender concerns in the mainstream of the state's overall development plan with one of the goals being, 'mainstreaming gender perspective in the development of processes, policies and programmes'. The policy aims to create an enabling environment for enjoyment of all human rights and fundamental freedom by women on equal basis with men in all spheres – personal, political, economic, social, cultural and civil. To address gender issues in private and public arenas, it aims towards a shared responsibility for children and home and step by step elimination of prejudices and practices that are gender discriminatory including the strengthening of legal systems. It also endeavors to eradicate all forms of violence against women and girl child.

To achieve these aims, it recommends multi-faceted approaches of gender sensitization, gender mainstreaming, gender planning, gender audit, gender analysis and gender convergence. Inter-sectoral partnerships and coalitions between departments, development of new institutional mechanisms, institutionalization of gender concerns in capacity building are the main operational strategies outlined by the policy for further strengthening gender mainstreaming within government. To achieve inter-sectoral convergence, the Nari Gaurav Niti has detailed action plans in eight key sectors. These detailed action plans consist of responsible department/agency, nodal agency and time frame to translate policy commitments into concrete actions. All departments are required to prepare a detailed plan with a focus on mainstreaming gender issues in their programmes and monitor the progress. Individual departments also maintain a beneficiary database for all the programs contributing towards women's development. As part of strengthening the Economic Environment for Women, Nari Gaurav Niti further recommends, "cover women under various beneficiary oriented programs from existing 30 to 50 per cent." According to this, each department is to ensure that 50 per cent of its physical and financial targets are set for women in all individual beneficiary oriented programs and schemes.

Key Programme/Scheme Achievements as per Nari Gaurav Niti

Economic Empowerment

- Formulation of about 2.24 lakh Sakhi Mandals (2011-12) leading to saving worth 181.38 crore and linkages built with Mission Mangalam for sustained economic development of members of the mandals.
- The widow pension scheme has provided 1,23,000 widows with monthly pension of 500 each and 80 per child (upto two children). 10,792 widows (age 18-40 years) given vocational training.
- 133 schools/colleges have a special guidance corner for women on career and job options.

- 50% of the total PDS shop permits given to Mahila Mandals.
- Leadership development trainings to Mahila Sarpanches have been established to support women candidates in Panchayat elections.
- Commissionerate, Women and Child Development has trained 53,123 women for economic empowerment.
- 23 women ITIs and 45 women wing in general ITI have been established.
- 50% seats are reserved for women under Craftsman Skill Development Programme.
- 6,299 urban BPL women employed under Urban Income Employment Programme.
- 61,310 women farmers received training in agriculture and 10,000 women farmers participated in Krishi Melas.

Housing

- 1.40 lakh houses built in the ownership of wife and 30,850 houses built in the joint ownership of husband and wife under Indira Awas Yojna (2010-11).
- Under Sardar Awas Yojna, 1.44 lakh houses were allotted in the name of women (2010-11).
- 1,41,822 plots were allotted to BPL Families and 67,654 SANAD were given to BPL Families (2009-11). The SANAD has been issued jointly in the name of wife and husband.

Governance

- 30% reservation for women in Government jobs with an increase in age limit by 5 years for women.
- 72,512 women are members on 17,773 Pani Samitis across Gujarat (33.9% Women).
- 4,93,149 women are members of 3,205 Participatory Forest Management Committees.
- 2,119 Women Milk Cooperatives are run with a membership of 6,42,208 women.

Health

- Rights of charter of patients displayed in all PHCs and CHCs.
- Quality Health Assurance Programme provided to approximately 95.06% PHCs with water facility and 96.08% with sanitation facility.
- 30,963 ASHA workers appointed in remote areas to address health concerns of women and children.

Some More Women-Specific Path Breaking Programmes and Schemes

- Property registration fees are exempted if property is registered in the name of women. Fee worth Rs. 473.50 crore were exempted by the Government benefitting 13.30 lakh women. (Annexure-12)
- The emergency response service – 108 has helped 8,26,930 pregnant women in accessing pregnancy related emergencies service whereas 22,682 women got emergency delivery services (delivery at scene and in ambulance). (Annexure-13)
- Mahila Police Stations and Mahila Police Cells have been established to help women in need.
- Government organizes Self Defense Training for programs. (Annexure-14)
- Government has provided crèche facility, which is free for Class-4 employees and also there are working women hostels. (Annexure-15)

The above is just a glimpse of many programs being run by the Government of Gujarat for the benefit of women and child development in Gujarat.

Moving from Second Curve to Third Curve depends on the lasting high performance in the Second Curve. For this the organizations must have insights which can provide 'threshold' to scale the Third Curve. This threshold can be an activity in isolation but essential part of women and child development. In a graph 'Threshold' will be represented with no more than a dot.

The threshold might look like just one element the 'dot' or 'bindu' but in reality lot is woven around it. In Gujarat, the Chaudhari tribals prepare a liquid out of jawar-flour and buttermilk with which they print their hands on agricultural implements, on cattle and also on their walls of their huts. They also draw figures on the walls and sprinkle this liquid on the walls. This sprinkling creates white dots on walls. For them its the act of feeding the walls. The tribals of Chhota Udaipur region in Gujarat, the 'Rathwas', offer the terracotta to their Gods. But they won't buy a terracotta horse, elephant, or tiger without the sprinklings of white dots on it. In the terracotta, dots themselves become the ultimate expression representing eyes, ears, breasts, nostrils, navel and sex organ.

If there are eight dots around a central dot, it becomes a 'kaudi' a unit of currency of Kutch Gujarat. 'Vagharis' women wear a cloth 'thapedu' which is red in colour with a pattern of white dot, created as a part of design on the fabric. Every design has a fix number of dots, any variation is not acceptable. In 'bandhani' print, it is the dot that converts an ordinary cloth into a priceless fabric. 'Chundadi', which is worn by the women of Gujarat in the marriages, is also designed with dots. In fact, a square piece of cloth with tie-dye dots, is offered to the Mother Goddess in which she adorns herself.

In fact across India, dot plays a very important role. In the Rangoli as well as Kolam, the dots guide all the patterns. A mole on a cheek is called 'sesame' seed i.e. 'til' which is always seen as an auspicious sign and also as an adornment of the body.

One cannot afford to forget the dot (the threshold point) in any way—it is no decoration separate from life: it is life itself (of the program).

The program which gives the threshold to move to Third Curve is called 'Chiranjeevi Yojna' which means 'a scheme for long life' (of mothers and babies).

Chiranjeevi Yojna: It is estimated that in the state of Gujarat about 1.2 million children are born each year. Some mothers who belong to Below Poverty Line (BPL) families are the most vulnerable to death during delivery since they face significant risk owing to their poor socio-economic status and limited access to healthcare services. The

Chiranjeevi Yojna implemented by the Government of Gujarat is a scheme for marginalized mothers to have free of cost delivery by skilled private practioners in a private nursing home.

The private Obstetricians and Gynecologists who wish to join the scheme sign an agreement with the Chief District Health Officer to conduct one hundred deliveries. For this the government pays the doctor a sum of Rs. 1,79,500. This figure has been worked out to include normal deliveries as well as cesarean sections.

Under the scheme, the mother gets free treatment during delivery including all the medicine. In addition she is paid out-of-pocket costs incurred on travel to reach the healthcare facility centre. (Annexure-16) Assistance of Rs. 200/- for transportation expenses with Rs. 50/- for the attendant who has accompanied her. Approximately, 1,63,609 women have availed the benefit of this scheme. (Graph-IX)

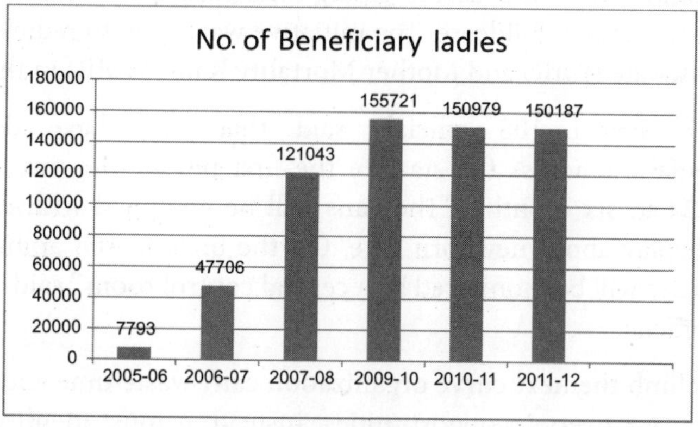

(Graph-IX)

The scheme has taken a next step through 'Khilkhilat' vans. On its launch, *The Times of India* on 6 September 2012 reported it as "When Geeta Rawal, 25, a resident of Saheb na Muvada village near Dehgam in Gandhinagar district was taken to a van two days after delivery of her first child, she could not believe that she was to be taken to her residence by this pink van free of cost. Rawal became the first mother to have availed the newly-launched service 'Khilkhilat' on Wednesday afternoon." As is the case with any new venture, we were excited to attend the first case. Rawal was admitted to the Gandhinagar civil hospital for her delivery. Her relatives did not know about the initiative and asked us that they would take her on their own. However, when they got about the free service and its benefits, they agreed readily. We took her from the hospital to her village and also provided her with nutrition kit for the newly-born. The kit also included list of vaccines to be given at specific times and information about nearby government hospitals," said an EMRI official.

'Khilkhilat', an ambulance for safe homecoming of infants and mothers post-delivery, was one of the three health schemes launched by Gujarat Chief Minister on September 4 at Mahatma Mandir in Gandhinagar. The ambulances are in fact vehicles that are phased out by the EMRI's flagship emergency service 108 after stipulated time of service. They have been renovated to suit the purpose and fitted with cushions and LCD screen giving information to the mother and her relatives about childcare. The initiative was taken to reduce Infant Mortality Rate (IMR) and Mother Mortality Rate (MMR) in the state.

GVK EMRI 108 officials said that they have deployed 20 ambulances across the state in the first phase. The number will reach 124 in six months. "The vans will be equipped with en route video display about newborn care. On the lines of 108 ambulances, the vehicles will be monitored by a central control room," said a senior EMRI official.

To climb the next curve organization can't waste time and money on small or uncertain opportunities. Instead, it must identify a "big enough development insight," that is, a substantial change on the horizon that heralds the chance to build a developed society for the organization that identifies and seizes the opportunity.

They build essential capabilities before scaling their operations and plan for success on Third Curve. Often focusing on details such as channel strategy early on, they understand exactly how they must be distinctive in order to create the value that society demands.

Government of Gujarat climbed the Third Curve of Women and Child Development through various initiatives. Some of them are:

- Tarun Sampark
- Mission Mangalam
- E–Mamta

Tarun Sampark

Traditionally men were left out of maternal and child health care approaches. Gujarat government realized the importance of men's shared responsibility and participation in reproductive healthcare. This role begins right from adolescence as only informed young men can fulfill the responsibility of mature husbands and fathers. Gujarat has designed the Tarun Sampark as a means for reaching out to adolescent boys.

So far principles of male development were casted as universal principle of human development. This is the first instance where male are being developed in their thinking and behavior for women and child development.

Mission Mangalam

Over time, Gujarat has emerged as the growth engine of India; its pace of economic growth continues to be higher than the national average. Along with this remarkable economic progress, Gujarat has given the country the formula of inclusive growth. Gujarat government strongly believes in the principle of uniform growth. After all no society, state or country can prosper, if only certain sections remain the constant beneficiaries of all the government schemes. Hence, to ensure that women in Gujarat are not disadvantaged and are equal to men in every possible way the State Government launched 'Mission Mangalam' on the occasion of the Golden Jubilee Year celebrations in 2010. Mission Mangalam is basically an integrated poverty alleviation approach in a demand driven convergence mode. It aims to channelise the critical mass of resources and mitigate poverty by creating a single platform for stakeholders. The idea is to integrate Sakhi Mandals (self-help groups) into the corporate value chain, thereby generating a win-win proposition for all the stakeholders. In the next three to five years, under Mission Mangalam, the state aims to create livelihoods for about a million people, in the rural sectors, through self-employment.

The objectives of this program are to mobilize the poor into collectives like Sakhi Mandals (SHGs) or Producer Groups (PGs) or Service Groups; nurture skills in them; assist them with microfinance and eventually empower them through sustainable livelihoods.

For the implementation of these objectives, the Government of Gujarat started the Gujarat Livelihoods Promotion Company (GLPC), a PPP (Public-Private-Partnership) company registered under the Companies Act 1956. GLPC has a strong team of around 150 professionals at State and District levels. These professionals are supported by 1800 field functionaries. There are various schemes for the rural poor involving available capital and interest subsidies. Some of these schemes have major elements of training and development linkages. The Schemes propose to integrate the SHGs or PGs in the corporate value chain with capital and interest subsidies and function as a PPP model. The preparation of the training proposal, training content, forward and backward market links and quality control is the responsibility of the private party. The GLPC works in tandem with the network of Sakhi Mandals or Self Help Groups (SHGs) and collaborates with large industries. So, strategic partnerships with banks, professional institutions, skill-development agencies, industry associations, etc. provide finance, skills and market information to SHGs.

Generally, in rural households women actively participate in and contribute to a large number of economic activities. But their contribution often goes unnoticed and their shares of profits are denied. But now this issue has been addressed with the launch of Mission Mangalam. The Sakhi Mandals can get in touch with Mission Mangalam officials and seek advice on a host of financial matters. The officials are not only glad to offer assistance but they also facilitate processes and transactions, e.g. the insurance process.

Mission Mangalam has around 2,38,937 operational Sakhi Mandals as on date, covering more than 29 lakh rural households. The bank savings of these Sakhi Mandals have reached the mark of Rs. 400 crores. Banks have extended credit support to the tune of Rs. 1,100 crores because of the proactive approach adopted by these SHGs.

Thus, an overall capital support of Rs. 1,500 crores has been made available to the Sakhi Mandals through Mission Mangalam. This has empowered the Sakhi Mandals to undertake economic activities in the form of micro-enterprises as the average fund availability has increased now to '62,500' per Sakhi Mandal as compared to just '18,000' prior to the launch of Mission Mangalam. Around 58,000 Sakhi Mandals have been graduated to meaningful micro-enterprise activities providing livelihood to more than 6 lakh rural households. The remaining are at various stages of social mobilisation activities, trainings and backward-forward market linkages.

For the empowerment and improvement of their economic and social status, creation of Sakhi Mandals has been undertaken since 2nd February 2007. Under this initiative, in order to promote economic self dependence and habit of saving some money for future, women members of Self Help Groups are motivated and engaged in income generation activities. The scheme is effectively implemented by the Department of Women and Child Development in convergence with the Department of Rural Development. With an aim of providing Revolving Fund grants along with loans, Government of Gujarat provides Rs. 1,500 per Sakhi Mandal group as a motivation.

In the Swarnim Gujarat year, with an objective of women empowerment and improving the Human Development Index especially among the poor through self economic generation activities; formation of Mission Mangalam has been undertaken. In the fifth summit of Vibrant Gujarat 2011 'Gujarat Livelihood Promotion Company' has signed a 57 Memorandum of Understanding with 32 corporate. On execution of these MoUs, within 3-5 years more than 15 lakhs women will receive employment. Statistically more than 2 lakh Sakhi Mandals are functional wherein 25 lakhs women have a saving of total Rs. 161.54 crore in banks proving success of the collective and teamwork efforts.

Benefits from the Vibrant Gujarat Summit (2011) Mission Mangalam has already triggered an overwhelming response from the business world resulting in MoUs (Memorandum of Understanding) worth more than Rs. 21,000 crores generating more that 1.4 million sustainable livelihoods. Some of the largest corporate houses in the country got involved in this process through the Vibrant Gujarat Summit, 2011. Immense interest and urge to partner with Mission Mangalam has been shown by corporate houses, banks and institutions understanding the strength of the collectives of the rural-poor households in the form of Sakhi Mandals. This initiative of Gujarat is a workable innovative model which is equipped with the most appropriate and effective strategy for poverty reduction in the post-liberalization era. It is a novel approach towards involving the corporate sector and the poor with an emphasis on skill development to transform the marginalized into successful entrepreneurs.

One must remember that this program is different than providing women with sales outlets for their handicraft projects. Training, loan and sales outlet for handicraft products are provided under Ghar Divda Scheme. (Annexure-17)

The Women Economic Development Corporation recommends the banks of respective areas to accept the application forms of the applicants for providing them loan up to Rs. 50,000/- for undertaking economic activities. It provides subsidy to Below Poverty Line women to establish micro-enterprise. For business subsidy Rs. 7,500/-, for Service subsidy Rs. 10,000/- and for small industries Rs. 12,500/- is provided. SC/ST are getting 40% subsidy, others get 20% subsidy, and for blind and disabled 50% subsidy is provided. Any woman whose family yearly income is below Rs. 36,000/- can apply for the benefit subject to the following eligibilities:

- She must be between 18 to 50 years of age.
- For the occupation as per the Corporation's list, she must be possessing necessary educational qualifications/experience certificate/hereditary business etc. for business.

Exhibition cum Sale to Support Women Artisans

Under this scheme Gujarat Women Economic Development Corporation Ltd (GWEDC) arranges (Annexure-18) exhibition cum sale and crafts bazaar for sustainable marketing support to sell the items produced by women or women self help groups is sold and in a way they are getting income. Exhibition cum sale are being organized by the corporation within state and out of the state. Women are provided either table space or stalls in the exhibition cum sale. Women get an opportunity to sell their products with minimum cost and get an experience of establishing long term linkages for marketing. But the high mark of this scheme was when last year i.e 2011, five women trained and funded under the scheme, got their stall in World Trade Fair held at New Delhi, and achieved a combined sales of more than Rs. 8 lakhs.

Mission Mangalam is a 'for profit' proposal and not a Corporate Social Responsibility (CSR) activity.

Innovative Use of Technology

Technology is really about enabling change and amplifying the direction that it takes. The direction of change isn't dictated by the technology; it's dictated by the choices – choices made by leadership. Technology enables workers to do what they couldn't do on their own in the past, which isn't so much a revolutions in technologies as it is a mind shift for workers and managers, a breakthrough in learning how to integrate technology and the worker.

SATCOM sessions (two way satellite communication) on various health nutrition topics are conducted to enable AWWs in carrying out the counseling sessions more efficiently. The SATCOM also helps in creating awareness amongst the community members on various health and nutrition issues.

Various SATCOM sessions had been organized last year on following topics:

a) Annaprashan and importance of appropriate complementary feeding.

b) IYCF (Infant and Young Child Feeding) Practices.

c) ENBC (Essential New Born Care).

d) Hand wash on Global Hand Washing Day etc.

Supervisors also sometimes make home visits, especially to houses of severely underweight children or those who need immediate attention.

Mother and Child Tracking System

The Health and Family Welfare Department of Gujarat has developed a name based mother and child tracking program in collaboration with National Informatics Centre to ensure service delivery so that none is left out. It is envisaged to strengthen monitoring of indicators for better implementation in order to reduce morbidity and mortality among mothers, children and adolescents.

SMS Alert are generated for all maternal and child services to beneficiaries as well as services providers. Gujarat is the only state with all 25 districts reporting in Routine Immunization Monitoring System.

The technology platform developed by Gujarat - E-Mamta, for tracking of pregnant mothers and children for assured services is now up scaled in entire Nation as Mother and Child Tracking System.

The Economic Times of 22 March 2012 had to say the following about the program:

India, where nearly 13 million infants die every year, is in the process of implementing nationally E-Mamta - a mobile phone based technology innovation conceptualised and first implemented by the Gujarat government in May, 2010.

In Gujarat, thousands of rural health workers, trained by the National Rural Health Mission (NRHM), go door-to-door collecting information on pregnant women, infants and sends it using their mobile phone to State Rural Health Mission (SRHM), the government body, which collates the data into a centralised repository. This data is then used to alert rural health workers - through SMS - to make sure they reach out to the pregnant women and mothers regarding immunisation dates or medicines to be taken.

"E-Mamta has been a great success in reaching out to rural families. In recent years, a large number of developing countries have combined mobile technology with public health delivery to communicate with the most remote person," says Dr Devi Prasad Shetty, founder of Narayana Hrudalaya hospital in Bangalore, and a poster-boy of success in healthcare innovation.

With the success in Gujarat, NRHM is piloting the model in others states. States such as Himachal Pradesh, Uttarakhand, Jammu & Kashmir and Jharkhand have rolled out E-Mamta with the help of National Informatics Council. The plan is to take it national eventually.

In Andhra Pradesh, the project is called Amma Lalana, which means mother's care in the local lingo. It is an initiative that tracks the health status of all pregnant women and infants through a cellphone based system. It goes a step ahead to get these women to make use of public health centers for free primary care instead of having to pay to go to a private facility.

"We have all this healthcare infrastructure and doctors from some of the best medical schools but people were still going to private hospitals and paying at least Rs. 5,000-10,000 for a delivery if not more," says Smita Sabharwal, collector and district magistrate at Karimnagar, which is the only district in the state to have taken it up. "We wanted to give them an alternative. It was really an exercise to put the faith back in the government…"

While E-Mamta appears to be a step in the right direction, there is still some disconnect – the absence of local script support for low-end mobile phones is proving to be a challenge. The messages right now sent are in the local language but typed in English alphabets. While most ANMs are trained and may have some level of comfort with English, it cannot be taken for granted.

One way of addressing it could be by sending recorded voice messages, which is being developed in Gujarat. "Recorded messages are easier to understand and there is no scope for ambiguity," Sabharwal said. According to Sharma, the NRHM is developing an automated voice response system which will speak to the beneficiaries in their regional languages and possibly put them in direct contact with the experts through a mobile hotline.

This year, E-Mamta won the Social Innovation Honours Awards given out every year by industry body Nasscom, which saw great potential in combining a network of trained health-workers along with mobile technology. "Besides its wide reach, E-Mamta will act as a tool for economic development," says Rita Soni, chief executive at Nasscom Foundation, industry body's arm that promotes technology for sustainable development.

Gujarat is the only state in India where all districts report in Routine Immunisation Monitoring System.

Both programs i.e. Mission Mangalam and E-Mamta shift the paradigm of development. One of the most important and effective components of Third Curve is Sakhi Mandal. It is important to note that Sakhi Mandal as a program was started in Second Curve. To visualize a second curve program to lead third curve development needs leadership that has vision, for inclusive growth.

There are indicators of each of the three curves (Table-14). But it is important to understand that there is no clear demarcation line as to where one curve ends and the next starts; there is always a overlap.

First Curve	Second Curve	Third Curve
The delivery system is designed to meet the needs of providers.	The delivery system is designed to be user-driven.	Incorporates needs of all: givers and users along the continuum.
The system, structures and process have evolved over time and have been cobbled together with unaligned assumptions in each department.	Systems, structures and process are aligned and intentionally designed to achieve the outcomes required.	Leadership alignment produces synergy within organization and across the delivery system.
System is fragmented, women fends for herself moving from department to department.	System is seamless, coordinates needs of women and child, using dedicated assistance to needy.	System reaches out to women and kid.
System, structures and process are designed to control and regulate the people working in the system.	System, structures and process are designed to facilitate collaboration, coordination and teamwork.	System, structures and process are designed to achieve right balance of empowerment and accountability.

First Curve	Second Curve	Third Curve
System, structures and process are designed to find out "Who is to blame".	Designed to produce collaborative behavior and teamwork.	Designed to experiment and explore new ways.
The system requires compliance from people.	The system seeks commitment from people.	People become the system.
Goal is to maximize resources for department.	Goal is to allocate resources within the system.	People allocate the resources themselves.
Traditional budgeting process are political, inflexible and linear.	Budgeting for fulfilling the obligation of the state	Gender Responsive Budgeting.
Governance represents the self interests of political party.	Governance represents the self interest of the organization.	Governance represents the 'owners': the citizens/ community.

(Table-14)

Amartya Sen in his inauguration lecture for the new Radcliffe Institute at Harvard University, on April 24, 2001 spoke on "Many faces of gender inequality" focusing on South Asia. He specified 'Seven Types of Inequality' which is as follows:

1. **Mortality inequality:** In some regions in the world, inequality between women and men directly involves matters of life and death, and takes the brutal form of unusually high mortality rates of women.
2. **Natality inequality:** Given a preference for boys over girls that many male-dominated societies have, gender inequality can manifest itself in the form of the parents wanting the newborn to be a boy rather than a girl.
3. **Basic facility inequality:** Even when demographic characteristics do not show much or any anti-female bias, there are other ways in which women can have less than a square deal. Where girls have far less opportunity of schooling than boys do. There are other deficiencies in basic facilities available to

women, varying from encouragement to cultivate one's natural talents to fair participation in rewarding social functions of the community.

4. **Special opportunity inequality:** Even when there is relatively little difference in basic facilities including schooling, the opportunities of higher education may be far fewer for young women than for young men. Indeed, gender bias in higher education and professional training can be observed even in some of the richest countries in the world, in Europe and North America.
5. **Professional inequality:** In terms of employment as well as promotion in work and occupation, women often face greater handicap than men. A country like Japan may be quite egalitarian in matters of demography or basic facilities, and even, to a great extent, in higher education, and yet progress to elevated levels of employment and occupation seems to be much more problematic for women than for men.
6. **Ownership inequality:** In many societies the ownership of property can also be very unequal. Even basic assets such as homes and land may be very asymmetrically shared. The absence of claims to property cannot only reduce the voice of women, but also make it harder for women to enter and flourish in commercial, economic and even some social activities. This type of inequality has existed in most parts of the world.
7. **Household inequality:** There are, often enough, basic inequalities in gender relations within the family or the household, which can take many different forms. It is, for example, quite common in many societies to take it for granted that while men will naturally work outside the home, women could do it if and only if they could combine it with various inescapable and unequally shared household duties.

Amartya Sen further makes the point under the heading 'What Women's Agency Can Achieve'; where he says: "There is, for example, plenty of evidence that whenever social and economic arrangements depart from the standard practice of male ownership, women can seize business and economic initiative with much success. It is also clear that the result of women's participation is not merely to generate income for women, but also to provide many other social benefits that come from women's enhanced status and independence."

The Three Curves have satisfactorily covered the issues raised by Amartya Sen and have delivered too. And have gone beyond too. In Gujarat, mother's name after child's name is necessary for registration in school.

Narendra Modi Model for Women and Child Development

'Women and Children Development' is complex and needs something more than a linear solution. Women, who constitute half the population, are caught in a vulnerable cycle of physical weakness, violence, illiteracy, poverty and marginalization to name a few.

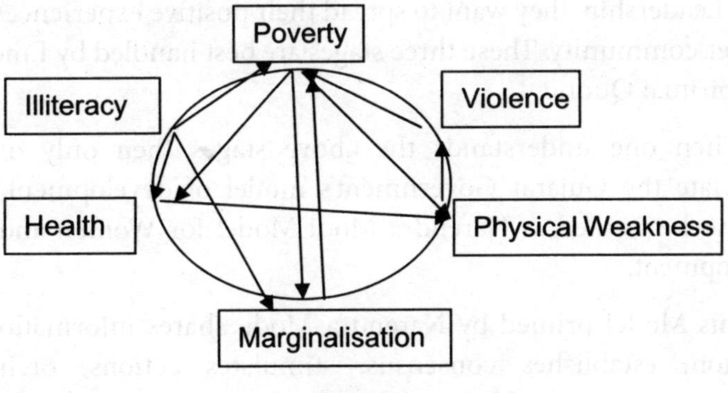

(Figure-2)

According to a study, the Development of Women has following stages:

- Powerlessness
- Initiation
- Participation
- Adoption, and
- Leadership

From among these stages of development, the first two stages of Powerlessness and Initiation are categorized to be passive, where women are not aware of the injustice they are facing, and do not speak up for their rights and needs. During these stages, women are just getting to know that they can achieve a better life for themselves and their families, what organizational interventions are about, and why they should attend the organizational interventions. Women passively interact and take part in organizational interventions during these two stages. These are essentially design issues of a program.

The other two stages of Participation and Adoption are considered to be active where women proactively get involved and seek interaction with organizational interventions, local agents, and other active women in the community. During these stages of development, women are interested in learning how to bring an improved life to themselves and their families, where they can seek help and resources, when they can start to achieve this development, and in the third stage i.e. of Leadership, they want to spread their positive experiences to the broader community. These three stages are best handled by Emotional and Spiritual Quotient.

When one understands the above stages then only one can appreciate the Gujarat Government's model of development which can also be termed as Narendra Modi Model for Women and Child Development.

This Model primed by Narendra Modi, shares information, sets direction, establishes consensus, stimulates actions, orchestrate processes, rewards, and balances long term and short term goals while revisiting conventional wisdoms. This model looks at the bigger picture of improving lives of the women in a holistic way. Model consider the society's and women's long-term professional and personal growth, while looking at how the solutions can help women escape the vicious cycles of discrimination, poverty, illiteracy, and unemployment, among others. Given the magnitude of problems associated with women's inequality, systematic progress can be made only by taking a holistic look, like: who are some of these women? What are some of their needs, challenges and aspirations? How do these characteristics vary with ascending levels of empowerment? How should we think holistically about designing appropriate programs, technologies to empower them?

It is not a linear model. It means constant evaluation and awareness of the big picture as well as awareness of the details of getting everyday business accomplished.

Criticisms of any government's initiatives are many. Sunil Krishna in Genderscapes writes: "In the post independence period, India's policy towards women was conventional and welfarist, clubbing women with children and the disabled. Since the 6th plan (1978-79 to 1982-83), there has been a more specific focus on women although this has lacked consistencies and has wavered between the earlier welfarist and the more recent 'instrumentalist' approaches. This is also so with regard to women and natural resources. ...Specific policies such as those for agriculture or water and the recent 10th plan document, as also state level initiatives, show that policy-makers are conscious of the lack of gender-equity. ...it is not women's empowerment that is the real focus of policy but rather the strengthening of women as the most effective instruments to improve family welfare, environmental conservation, and wasteland regeneration and so on. Such an approach has been called the 'efficiency' argument but I prefer to use the term 'instrumentalist' because it more clearly shows where the focus lies.

...The New Agricultural policy, 2000, which is the part of the 10th plan, is explicit about the instrumental rational of giving women land rights (see also Rao 2005): "Strengthening the conditions of female farmers and female labourers would also help improve the food security at the household level. This is because generally women spend most of their income on household expenditure unlike men and this would help improve the nutrition of the children."

Likewise, the plan chapter on environment and forests states that rural people, particularly women and tribal communities, have an intimate knowledge of species, their growth characteristics, utility, individual value etc. It says this knowledge is 'utilised' for the community under Joint Forest Management. In the past, similar arguments have also been explicitly put forward regarding professional women forest officers; the forest service could use them as instruments to carry the message of forest protection to village women, and through them to village communities.

At the state level too similar sentiments are expressed. The intention is clear: increase women's management of resources to improve conservation and family welfare.

The equity concerns that are sprinkled through policy statements and the program document effectively masked the reinforcement of women's traditional roles and the release of men from responsibilities from household, food provisioning and community resource conservation.

The Planning Commission midterm appraisal of the 10th plan is also revealing: it lists 59 priority actions that it says could yield results immediately. …Gender concerns are not separately addressed in any of this priority action…

Given this policy scenario it is not at all surprising that women's empowerment has been far from being the focus of modern scientific resource management. "...Their productive participation in the household and larger economy, and their contribution to the conservation and sustainability of resources, is either ignored by policy makers or appropriated in instrumentalist ways."

But these criticism doesn't hold true for Narendra Modi's Model. Gujarat Government's programs have always seen women as Shakti. In fact it will be safe to say that Government of Gujarat is ahead of the challenges which might develop due to changing world scenario and related criticism. For example, feminist scholars have long challenged the view that there is a positive correlation between political and economic liberalization (Elson 1989, Afshar and Dennis 1991). They have argued that the increased pressure arising from economic liberalization are exacerbating the burden that women carry in their daily lives and therefore reducing the time and space for them to be politically active. (The Gender Politics of Development, Shirin M. Rai). In Gujarat Mission Mangalam empowers women as well as Samras Panchayat schemes takes women's participation in politics to next level. Not to forget that "Gujarat is the first state to pass women's empowerment Bill for 50% reservation in local bodies, but denied assent despite Governor being a woman."

This model helps leaders observe transformation from success to failure and take remedial measures. It also helps identify new programs which will help the organization to jump to next curves of growth and development.

As women attain more equality of Control in factors of production and distribution of benefits, they can gain more equality in Welfare (such as in food supply, income, and health care). While this model informs priority areas of gender equality to focus on for developmental interventions, this model also emphasize design directions, and does provide an understanding of the actual external contexts and practical situations faced during grass-roots development work such as the actual stakeholders, intra-family and intra-community social interactions and socio-cultural dynamics, organizational best practices harnessed, problems faced at each stage by the stakeholders, and other practical details that are necessary for women's development and empowerment.

Success mantra of this model is that it is an integrated model of long-term development at the grassroots. Thinking behind Policies and Programs of this model is that enhanced status of women is an index of growth of a society and civilization. It has been done by inspiring the bureaucracy and giving them secure tenures to implement policies on the ground.

Women and Child Development is a lesser known story about Gujarat, compared to its industrial and infrastructural prowess. While in reality it is Women and Child Development, which actually makes Narendra Modi and the State of Gujarat hard to beat.

One of the critics about Women's Development program, Prabha Kishore writes: "I feel that the whole purpose behind the government running these programs is that it can create a pool of sensible women voters. The need a women who can vote sensibly and who can talk – so that the government can say to the world, 'see our women are so empowered.'"

Even this criticism doesn't hold good in case of Gujarat.

Narendra Modi asks mahila sarpanchs to work as CMs or PMs of villages: In a function held at Gujarat University convention hall in Ahmedabad Chief Minister Narendra felicitated 831 female sarpanchs of Samras village panchayats and gave away incentive prizes worth Rs. 22.50 crore.

Chief Minister said that women in villages have already proved their leadership guts by effectively managing water distribution work through WASMO and by being successful in dairy and animal husbandry industry. The female sarpanchs have all the strengths required to bring grassroots changes in villages. They should feel as if they are the chief ministers or prime ministers of their area and should effectively manage the panchayat administration....

"As many as 250 village panchayats have become Samras entirely. It is unique and commendable that males of these villages have given a way to women for taking charge of panchayat administration. This will infuse villages with fresh vigor," ascertained the Chief Minister.

Referring to Mission Mangalam and Sakhi Mandals Chief Minister said that with such unique steps the state government has helped around 2.5 lakh rural women to get free from the shackles of debt and other financial problems by their economical empowerment.

This was possible because of "Leadership development trainings to Mahila Sarpanchs have been established to support women candidates in Panchayat elections" under Nari Gaurav Niti.

Not only this, in Gujarat percentage of women voters went up in the state from 57% in 2007 to 68.9%. Now women decide on their own whom to vote for, unlike in the past when the head of the family or their husbands used to decide for them.

According to Shri Narendra Modi, "This is an era of quantum leaps in development. This is an era of ensuring and securing active participation of the Woman Power in Development." Empowered women can contribute significantly towards the overall development of women in the State. Under this scheme the State Government gives rewards to villages where panchayat members are elected with consent so that elections can be avoided. The objective of Samras is to avoid inter-village enmities which the election politics create. The reward amount is Rs. 3 lakh for all women panchayats in villages with a population below 5,000 and Rs. 5 lakh for those with more than 5,000 people. Out of 2,147 villages that opted for the Samras scheme, 254 have elected only women as panchayat members, including the Sarpanch. "The number of such all-women panchayats has risen from 20 in the last elections to 254 this time," said Deputy Rural Development Commissioner. (Source PTI)

The above statement of Chief Minister calling women to take leadership role actually makes the whole women and child development initiative unique and justified to be termed as 'Narendra Modi Model of Women and Child Development' instead of 'Third Curve of Development'.

Apart from being in the 'third curve' of 'Development of Women and Child Development', the wide acceptance of the development initiatives taken by the Government of Gujarat by Central and Various State Governments across India establishes the fact that the initiatives have gone beyond statistics and have become a full-fledged model which needs to be documented, studied, taught and implemented.

Je Kar Jhulave Parnum, Te Jagatnum Shaasan Kare

– Gujarati Proverb

(The hand that rocks the cradle rules the world)

Annexure

Annexure-1 : Women's Participation in Gujarat Government

Department	Total Male Employees	Total Female Employees	Total	% of Female Employees
Education	7950	14655	22606	64.83
Health & Family Welfare	7971	9022	16993	53.09
Women and Child Development	84	48	132	36.36
Social Justice	2258	850	3108	27.35
General Government Office	67	18	85	21.18
Finance	5701	1322	7012	18.85
Narmada	454	103	557	18.49
Schedule Tribe Development Tribe	1038	225	1263	17.81
Parliamentary Affairs	51	9	60	15.00
Labour & Employment	5522	916	6438	14.23
Sports, Youth & Culture	912	133	1034	12.85
Food, Consumer	2056	215	2271	9.47
Industry	2355	222	2577	8.61
Road & House	6491	590	7081	8.33
Science & Technology	21	2	22	4.55
Port & Transport	43298	842	44140	1.91
Total	**86194**	**29162**	**11533**	**25.28**

Annexure-2A : Women Sewing Centers, Schedule Tribe

Year	Sewing Training Center	No. of Women Training Center	No. of Women Who were Paid Stipend	Total Amount of Stipend in Lakhs	No. of Women Beneficiary for Machine	Total Amount in Lakhs for Machine	Total Expense in Lakhs
2002-03	11	308	306	4.61	108	1.89	6.50
2003-04	11	337	337	4.85	183	3.54	8.39
2004-05	10	317	317	4.47	137	2.89	7.37
2005-06	10	256	254	3.75	53	1.06	4.81
2006-07	8	239	239	3.55	153	3.06	6.61
2007-08	7	199	199	2.95	53	1.50	4.45
2008-09	5	131	132	1.89	20	0.60	2.49
2009-10	2	100	100	1.09	0	0	1.09
2010-11	1	28	28	0.23	0	0	0.23
Total	**65**	**1915**	**1911**	**27.42**	**707**	**14.55**	**41.97**

Annexure-2B : Women Sewing Centers, Schedule Tribe/Schedule Caste

Year	Sewing Training Center	No. of Women Trained	No. of Women Who were Paid Stipend	Total Expense in Lakhs
2001-02	12	480	480	26.36
2002-03	12	480	480	25.72
2003-04	13	520	520	29.38
2004-05	13	520	520	27.64
2005-06	12	480	480	27.57
2006-07	12	480	480	28.88
2007-08	12	480	480	31.43
2008-09	12	480	480	28.67
2009-10	12	480	480	38.57
2010-11	12	480	480	31.54
Total	**122**	**4880**	**4880**	**294.76**

Annexure-3

Year	No. of MPWWC	No. of Female Beneficiary	Total Expense in Lakhs
2006-07	134	75834	79.01
2007-08	134	292326	205.58
2008-09	221	412280	305.00
2009-10	212	551635	370.10
Total	**701**	**1242075**	**950.69**

Annexure-3A : Subsidy to Women for Fishing Equipments

Year	No. of Female Scholarship Beneficiary	Expense in Lakhs
2003-04	563	10.04
2004-05	554	10.26
2005-06	461	8.66
2006-07	396	13.35
2007-08	189	4.92
2008-09	294	7.60
2009-10	147	5.66
2010-11	314	10.04
2011-12	194	3.86
Total	**3110**	**74.4**

Annexure-3B : Scheme for Women for Fisheries

Year	No. of Female Beneficiary	Expense in Lakhs
2004-05	268	11.45
2005-06	358	16.82
2006-07	431	17.46
2007-08	447	16.00
2008-09	458	16.58
2009-10	479	30.11
2010-11	507	30.48
2011-12	498	39.21
Total	**3416**	**178.11**

Annexure-4A : Kunverbai nu Mameru Scheme Schedule Tribe

Year	No. of Female Beneficiary	Expense in Lakhs
2001-02	2404	120.16
2002-03	2449	122.42
2003-04	3209	159.18
2004-05	4348	218.80
2005-06	4150	209.65
2006-07	4087	204.53
2007-08	3326	166.31
2008-09	2681	134.40
2009-10	1991	99.62
2010-11	1785	86.04
Total	**30430**	**1521.11**

Annexure-4B : Kunverbai nu Mameru Scheme Schedule Caste

Year	No. of Female Beneficiary	Expense in Lakhs
2001-02	4701	222.50
2002-03	2755	137.55
2003-04	6967	348.35
2004-05	6646	332.32
2005-06	4888	244.40
2006-07	4864	243.28
2007-08	4626	231.31
2008-09	2618	130.92
2009-10	3278	163.93
2010-11	2824	141.21
Total	**44167**	**2195.77**

Annexure-4C : Kunverbai nu Mameru Scheme Other Caste

Year	No. of Female Beneficiary	Expense in Lakhs
2001-02	8564	434.20
2002-03	6551	325.39
2003-04	7802	405.96
2004-05	6843	342.14
2005-06	3919	195.24
2006-07	3186	159.85
2007-08	4136	209.92
2008-09	4157	207.83
2009-10	4331	217.52
2010-11	4928	247.74
2011-12	3446	172.85
Total	**57863**	**2918.64**

Annexure-5 : Sakhi Mandal

Year	No. of Sakhi Mandal	No. of Members	Total Savings in Lakhs	Revenue Generated/ Year in Lakhs
2008	43777	593659	1252.4	1713
2009	97783	1275365	1590.2	12880
2010	169284	2087032	15847.2	33849
2011	199509	2437999	23657.4	46213
2012	201012	2455337	30101.86	32613
Total	**711366**	**8849392**	**72448.94**	**127268**

Annexure-6 : Vidyla Laxmi Bond

Year	No. of Schools	No. of Girl Child in School	No. of Girl Child Beneficiary	Total Investment in Crores
2002-03	32742	110829	110829	11.08
2003-04	32742	154457	154457	15.44
2004-05	32742	130000	130000	13.00
2005-06	32742	151034	151034	15.10
2006-07	32742	146200	146200	14.62

2007-08	32742	147506	147506	14.75
2008-09	32742	128757	128757	12.87
2009-10	32742	111553	111553	11.15
2010-11	32742	104317	104317	10.43
2011-12	32742	102598	102598	10.23
Total	**32742**	**1287251**	**1287251**	**128.7**

Annexure-7A : Vidya Sadhna Yojna

Year	No. of Beneficiary	Total Investment
2001-02	8275	96.32
2002-03	1878	20.82
2003-04	35197	528.00
2004-05	15753	236.39
2005-06	19863	290.91
2006-07	20550	308.46
2007-08	22600	451.13
2008-09	29804	597.14
2009-10	29448	586.52
2010-11	20447	670.82
Total	**212815**	**3789.61**

Annexure-7B : Saraswati Sadhna Yojna

Year	No. of Beneficiary	Total Investment
2001-02	42123	520.17
2002-03	38566	694.18
2003-04	11800	156.00
2004-05	3781	56.71
2005-06	3510	52.65
2006-07	3669	55.02
2007-08	4484	67.37
2008-09	4433	88.66
2009-10	5111	102.23
2010-11	3795	75.91
Total	**121264**	**1868.90**

Annexure-8 : Widow Insurance

Year	No. of Widows Covered	No. of Claims	Claim Amount in Lakhs	Premium Paid by Govt. in Lakhs
2008-09	109835	1	1	4.21
2009-10	117364	2	2	5.00
2010-11	123636	-	-	6.00
2011-12	121354	-	-	6.00
Total	**472189**	**3**	**3**	**21.21**

Annexure-9 : Scholarship to Female Sportspersons

Year	No. of Female Scholarship Beneficiary	Expenses in Lakhs
1999-00	731	31.30
2000-01	917	38.32
2001-02	669	28.93
2002-03	686	29.67
2003-04	561	23.96
2004-05	687	30.56
2005-06	822	36.57
2006-07	689	31.44
2007-08	651	29.18
2008-09	1853	81.00
2009-10		
2010-11	977	43.56
2011-12	1390	61.04
Total	**10633**	**465.53**

Annexure-10 : Types of Cases Heard in Nari Adalat

Types of Cases Heard in Nari Adalat	07-08	08-09	09-10	10-11	11-12
Divorce	52	46	52	22	75
Child Custody	41	19	29	17	13
Maintenance	27	21	32	14	3
Women not going to In-laws place	53	89	89	7	16
Mental-Physical Torture	267	187	301	626	464

Husband Not Calling the Woman	128	49	60	75	26
Parents married and child custody	38	4	16	0	4
Stree Dhan	20	24	24	32	74
Land Related	2	4	6	40	64
Others (Dowry, Witch Hunting, Rope, Extra marital affair etc.)	0	0	0	335	349
Total	**638**	**443**	**619**	**1168**	**1088**

Annexure-11 : Kanya Kelavani Rath Yatra and Shala Praveshotsav

Year	Boys	Girls	Total	Expense in Lakhs
2003-04	348989	313693	662682	223.55
2004-05	108834	104498	213332	113.79
2005-06	118728	116357	235085	134.37
2006-07	338567	307280	645847	463.71
2007-08	323294	297859	621154	533.72
2008-09	320104	299219	619323	727.60
2009-10	346583	321330	667913	971.05

Annexure-12 : Documents Registered under Female's Name

Year	No. of Properties Registered	No. of Properties Registered in Females Name	No. of Properties Registered in Females Name in %	Benefit to Women in Lakhs
2004	228511	51230	22	10.30
2005	500494	107199	21	18.76
2006	625461	106249	17	35.82
2007	680171	147572	22	37.75
2008	826230	187006	23	47.41
2009	676161	130371	19	42.13
2010	977810	184861	19	72.37
2011	937448	169711	18	98.92
2012	878859	154497	18	96.49
Total	**6331145**	**1238696**	**20**	**459.95**

Annexure-13 : 108 Emergency Mobile Service

Year	Mobile Vans	No. of Cases Registered	No. of Ladies Complaint	No. of Ladies Benefited	No. of Pregnancy Related Cases	No. of Deliveries in Van	Expense in Lakhs
07-08	76	38453	12537	12529	4009	222	451.83
08-09	380	513759	265919	265840	161400	4548	3255.13
09-10	451	770907	433650	433326	262499	7079	4162.76
10-11	451	797134	449305	449248	270714	8416	5268.69
11-12	506	751590	421788	421751	261976	8260	5269.05
12-13**	518	583424	359617	356577	221391	6229	2831.18*
Total	**518**	**3455264**	**1942531**	**1939271**	**1181990**	**34754**	**21238.64**

** upto February 2013 *upto September 2013

Annexure-14 : Self Defense Training Program for Women

Year	No. of Females Trained	Expense in Lakhs
2000-01	4380	4.24
2001-02	4404	4.12
2002-03	3154	2.56
2003-04	7411	6.17
2004-05	5659	7.26
2005-06	5564	6.30
2006-07	3059	6.48
2007-08	3569	7.33
2008-09	5021	9.39
2009-10	5466	5.02
2010-11	5466	5.02
Total	**47676**	**55.85**

Annexure-15 : Working Women Hostel

Year	No. of Women Benefited By Working Women's Hostel
2001	1851
2002	2067
2003	2077
2004	2127
2005	2085
2006	2185
2007	2135
2008	2254
2009	2185
2010	2212
2011	2256

Annexure-16 : Chiranjivee Yojna

Year	No. of Lady Ob Gyn	Beneficiary Ladies	Expense in Lakhs
2005-06	215	7793	98.54
2006-07	742	47706	886.8
2007-08	865	121043	2348.82
2009-10	721	155721	2919.74
2010-11	662	150979	3521.23
2011-12	646	150187	3410.56
2012-12 (till Jan 13)	475	71842	2011.58
Total		**840977**	**15310.98**

Annexure-17 : Ghar Divda Scheme

Year	No. of Females Scholarship Beneficiary	Expense in Lakhs
2000-01	1591	59.37
2001-02	1417	60.38
2002-03	1495	65.15
2003-04	996	49.02
2004-05	2246	104.88
2005-06	2838	113.50
2006-07	2551	125.90
2007-08	2145	135.75
2008-09	2480	161.01
2009-10	957	58.68
2010-11	1989	125.89
2011-12	1137	79.83
Total	**21842**	**1139.36**

Annexure-18 : No. of Exhibition

Year	No. of Females Beneficiary	Expense in Lakhs
2000-01	260	3.86
2001-02	173	2.6
2002-03	176	2.74
2003-04	99	1.97
2004-05	68	3.48
2005-06	156	7.29
2006-07	153	8.99
2007-08	5	9.57
2008-09	116	45
2009-10	0	0
2010-11	1	5.20
Total	**1207**	**90.7**

Reference

1. A Study of Nari Adalats (Women's Courts) and Caste Panchayats in Gujarat; Sushma Iyengar; UNDP; 2007
2. Ambaji temple takes up fight against child malnutrition; Pramod Panwar; The Times of India; 6 April 2011
3. Annual Programme Implementation Plan, 2011-12; Deptt. of Women and Child Development; Government of Gujarat
4. Bindu: The Dot Personified; Haku Shah, Design Thoughts; July 2009
5. Caste as Woman; Vrinda Nabar; Penguin Books; 1995
6. Creating Better Futures; James A. Ogilvy; Oxford; 2002
7. Designing and Creating 'Second Curve' Healthcare Systems; Ted Ball, Martin D. Merry, M.D. and Liz Verlaan-Cole
8. Educate the girl child; Ruchira Sen; CCS Working Paper no. 183; Summer Research Internship Programme 2007-08; Centre for Civil Society
9. Education for Women's Empowerment: An Evaluation of the Government run Schemes
10. E-Mamta: Gujarat's mobile tech helps reduce infant & maternal mortality, to be adopted across the nation; The Economic Times; 22 March 2012
11. Emotional Design; Donald A. Norman; Basic Books; 2004
12. Emotional Intelligence; Daniel Goleman; Bantam; 1996
13. Empowerment of Women Through Convergence Technology; U. Jerinabi & G. Santhiyavalli; Delhi Business Review, Vol. 2, No. 2, July-December 2001
14. Genderscapes; Sumi Krishna; 2008
15. Gujarat Widow Entrepreneurs; R.S. Patel, The Gujarat, Vol. II, Issue-1, January 2012
16. Gujarat on the road to Golden Health; Department of Health & Family Welfare, 2011

17. http://www.unicef.org/India/education_789.htm
18. Judgment; Noel M. Tichy & Warren G. Bennis; Portfolio, 2007
19. Mamta Abhiyan: Delivering Convergent Services for Improved Maternal and Child Health; Briefing Paper Series: Innovations, Lessons and Good Practices; UNICEF; 2011
20. Mission Mangalam Empowering Gujarat's Women; The Gujarat; Vol. II, Issue-2, April 2012
21. Nari Gaurav Niti, Sangeeta Singh; The Gujarat, Vol. II, Issue-1, January 2012
22. Paradoxes of Empowerment; Aradhana Sharma; Zubaan; 2010
23. Saving mothers and newborns through an innovative partnership with private sector obstetricians: Chiranjeevi scheme of Gujarat, India; Dileep Mavalankar, Amarjit Singh, Sureshchandra R. Patel, Ajesh Desai, Prabal V. Singh; International Journal of Gynecology and Obstetrics 107 (2009) 271-276
24. Shala Praveshotsav Kanya Kelavani; Sahil Jhingon; Vol. II; Issue-3, July 2012
25. Socio-Economic Review, 2011-2012, Gujarat State; Directorate of Economics And Statistics; Government of Gujarat, 2012
26. Speech of Narendra Modi, Chief Minister, Gujarat at the annual plan discussion in the planning commission, N. Delhi, 24 June 2011
27. Statistics on Women in India, 2012; NIPCCD
28. Subhash Chandra Bose – Pioneer of Indian Planning; Planning Commission, 1971
29. The Cycle of Leadership; Noel M. Tichy & Nancy Cardwell; Harper Collins, 2004
30. The Dynasty – A Political Biography of the Premier Ruling Family of Modern India; S.S. Gill, Rupa & Co, 2004
31. The Gender Politics of Development; Shirin M. Rai; Zuban; 2008
32. The Gujarat Miracle, The Sunday Guardian, New Delhi; 8 January 2012
33. The Second Curve; Ian Morrison; Ballantine Books; 1996
34. The Second Cycle; Lars Kolind; Wharton School Publishing; 2006
35. Women Deliver for Development; Kiran Gill, Rohini Pande and Anuj Malhotra; The Women Deliver Conference; 18-20 October 2007
36. Working With Emotional Intelligence; Daniel Goleman; Bantam Books; 1999

Rs 595

5